# Introduction

All too often, evangelization seems to be something else one has to add to an already busy schedule. It is not. It is the re-awakening of the "why" in what we already do. It is also a defining moment for us as disciples of Jesus Christ. For there is no discipleship without evangelization, and there is no evangelization without disciples.

*Ministry Through the Lens of Evangelization* celebrates the link between ministry and discipleship and contains the major presentations of the first North American Institute for Catholic Evangelization (NAICE) in 2003.

The development of NAICE began in 2000 with a proposal to the U.S. Commission on Catholic Evangelization, on behalf of the Archdiocese of Portland in Oregon by Deacon Thomas Gornick and myself, on behalf of the USCCB Secretariat for Evangelization.

The fundamental vision flowed out of Pope Paul VI's *Evangelii Nuntiandi: On Evangelization in the Modern World* (EN) and *Go and Make Disciples: A National Plan and Strategy for Catholic Evangelization in the United States* (GMD) by the United States Conference of Catholic Bishops (USCCB). All ministries must be seen through the lens of evangelization as the essential mission of the Church.

The United States Commission on Catholic Evangelization (USCCE) unanimously recommended to the USCCB Committee on Evangelization that such an institute take place. Under Bishop Michael Warfel's leadership at that time, the committee enthusiastically proposed that the first NAICE take place in Portland, Oregon in the summer of 2003. Bishop Edward Slattery, Bishop Warfel's successor as chairman, and the current Committee on Evangelization continue to support this latest initiative in nurturing the essential mission of the Church.

NAICE was built on two phases. Phase I was designed for Church leadership on the national, diocesan, and parish levels and took place at the University of Portland July 9-12, 2003. In addition to networking and time together, there were three major components to this institute: major presentations, table discussions, and panel responses. All participants were either assigned to a parish leadership table or a diocesan/national leadership table, which they kept for the duration of the institute. In this way, each table's leadership could begin to address challenges and hopes on a deeper level and be a supportive presence to one another in their networking after Portland.

Phase II of NAICE is for the local churches. Hopefully, participants in Phase I will sponsor a series of presentations similar to NAICE in their local dioceses using diocesan resources. This book of major presentations from NAICE 2003, *Ministry Through the Lens of Evangelization*, is an additional resource.

Recognizing the complexity of such an initiative, three essential components were needed in establishing this first institute: a diocese with active evangelization initiatives, a Catholic institution of higher learning committed to evangelization, and the support of the bishops. The three partners for NAICE 2003 were the Archdiocese of Portland in Oregon, the University of Portland, and the USCCB Committee on Evangelization with its U.S. Commission on Catholic Evangelization. Because of Portland's close proximity to Canada, the Archdiocese of Vancouver, British Columbia was invited to be a co-sponsor.

The theme for NAICE 2003 was *Ministry Through the Lens of Evangelization*. During NAICE, 457 disciples gathered from Canada, Colombia, Costa Rica, Honduras, Mexico, the North Mariana Islands, the United Kingdom, and the United States of America. From the United States, participants came from four eparchies and 107 dioceses, including the Archdiocese for Military Service, and from forty-one states, including Alaska and Hawaii, plus the District of Columbia.

The goal of a diverse representation from a variety of ministries was achieved. Men numbered 231 and women 226. Participants were divided into 151 in parish leadership, 196 in diocesan leadership, and 110 in national leadership. Slightly more than half the participants were lay men and women (273). Also present were twenty bishops, twelve deacons, and 108 priests, including four provincials and one congregation president. Through the support of the USCCB Secretariat for the Church in Latin America, a delegation from Latin America added to the richness of the diversity of the Church in America.

Another exciting dimension of NAICE 2003 was that it was promoted completely through the Internet and through the invitations of the diocesan evangelization coordinators. These coordinators invited participants from their dioceses, and no brochure was used for promotion or registration.

*Ministry Through the Lens of Evangelization* presents the major presentations and homilies given during the four days in Portland. Theodore Cardinal McCarrick addressed the theme of the institute in his keynote address. Other major presentations were on evangelization and culture; evangelization and media; evangelizing catechesis; Catholic youth and young adults in evangelizing efforts; evangelizing witness; evangelizing spirituality; and the centrality of the Word of God in the essential mission of the Church.

Reflection questions on all these subjects are available at the end of each major presentation. I want to express our gratitude to the delegations from the Archdiocese of Cincinnati and the Diocese of Albany for formulating the questions.

It is the hope of the USCCB Secretariat for Evangelization that *Ministry Through the Lens of Evangelization* will assist Catholic leadership in further implementing *Go and Make Disciples: A National Plan and Strategy for Catholic Evangelization in the United States* throughout all of the Church in America.

**John E. Hurley, CSP, D.Min**
*Executive Director*
Secretariat for Evangelization
United States Conference of Catholic Bishops

# Sponsors

**NAICE 2003 SPONSORS**
- The Archdiocese of Portland in Oregon
- The University of Portland
- The USCCB Committee on Evangelization and its U.S. Commission on Catholic Evangelization

**NAICE 2003 CO-SPONSOR**
- The Archdiocese of Vancouver, British Columbia

**NAICE 2003 PLANNING COMMITTEE**
*Archdiocese of Portland in Oregon*
- Deacon Thomas Gornick (General Coordinator)
- Bud Bunce
- Todd Cooper
- Sr. Jeremy Gallet, SP
- Michal Horace
- Randy Kollars
- Cathy Shannon

*Archdiocese of Vancouver*
- Msgr. Stephen Jensen

*University of Portland:*
- Very Rev. David Tyson, CSC
- Dr. Marlene Moore
- Rev. Edwin Obermiller, CSC
- William Reed

*USCCB Secretariat for Evangelization and*
*U.S. Commission for Catholic Evangelization*
- Rev. John Hurley, CSP (General Coordinator)
- Rev. Joseph Kruszynski, OFM Conv
- Rev. Paul Minnihan

*The sponsors and planning committee would like to express their gratitude to their support staffs and the following, for without their help and support, NAICE 2003 would not have been possible:*

## FOUNDATION SPONSORS
- The Clark Foundation of Oregon
- The Koch Foundation
- USCCB Secretariat for the Church in Latin America

## GENERAL SESSION SPONSORS
- Catholic Campaign for Human Development
- Christlife Catholic Evangelization Solutions
- Education for Parish Service
- Loyola Press
- Oregon Catholic Press
- The Paulist Fathers
- Paulist National Catholic Evangelization Association
- William H. Sadlier, Inc.
- USCCB

## PANEL SPONSORS
- Catholic Communications Campaign
- Little Rock Scripture Study
- Liturgical Press
- Loyola Institute for Ministry
- National Conference for Catechetical Leadership
- North American Forum on the Catechumenate
- Paulist Landings International
- Paulist Media Works
- Paulist Press
- Renew International
- St. Mary's Press
- Satellite Theological Education Program

# Keynote Address

## THE CALL TO A NEW EVANGELIZATION

Cardinal Theodore E. McCarrick • *Archdiocese of Washington, D.C.*

A
s the youngsters used to say, "This is very scary." I'm speaking about this awesome opportunity to talk to you about evangelization, to talk to you about the extraordinary privilege we have of proclaiming the message of the Good News of Jesus, to remind you that we are all called to be missionaries, to plumb the depths of our consciousness in Christ and to hear him call us once again to go out into the whole world and make disciples of every person.

It reminds me of that wonderful story that Archbishop Edwin O'Brien of the Military Archdiocese told the bishops at our meeting in St. Louis last month. He told a story that is apparently attributed to Blessed Pope John XXIII. As the story goes, when Pope John was serving as Apostolic Nuncio in the Balkans, he visited one of the bishops who lived in a rather ostentatious palace that he had inherited from his predecessors of centuries before. After the dinner, the bishop took the Nuncio around and showed him the beauty of the residence.

Somewhat sheepishly, at the end of the visit, the bishop turned to the future John XXIII and said, "So, Your Excellency, you can see that I cannot say, 'Gold and silver I have none.'" And, according to the story, the future Pope turned to him and with a sigh said, "Neither can you say, 'Rise up, pick up your bed, and walk!'"

I find myself in the position where I have neither the gold and silver of eloquence and profound learning, nor the deep spirituality that makes some of us into workers of miracles. That's why I want to say right at the beginning that I need you to pray with me that I will say this evening what the Lord wants me to say and that he will guide me to make sure that what I will say is what you need to hear as you begin this challenging experience in modern American Catholic evangelization.

> "We wish to confirm once more that the task of evangelizing all people constitutes the essential mission of the Church."
>
> Declaration of the Synod Fathers on Evangelization
> *L'Osservatore Romano,*
> October 27, 1974, p.6 (EN, no.14)

I know how important a missionary heart, a missionary consciousness, and a missionary zeal must be. You all know it too; that's why you're here. Over the past many years you have heard the Church say again and again, "We must be missionary." You have heard Paul VI speak in that magnificent apostolic exhortation *Evangelii Nuntiandi: On Evangelization in the Modern World (EN)* of 1975 in which he sets out so clearly, so forcefully and so beautifully the whole philosophy and theology of the mission apostolate. Let me just quote from No. 14 of that exhortation:

> We wish to confirm once more that the task of evangelizing all people constitutes the essential mission of the Church. It is a task and mission which the vast and profound changes of present-day society make all the more urgent. Evangelizing is in fact the grace and vocation proper to the Church, her deepest identity. She exists in order to evangelize.[1]

No one could have it said more forcefully than that, or more clearly. It is not possible for us to exist as a Catholic people unless we evangelize. This means that we must evangelize whatever we do and wherever we are. We cannot be Church without being missionary. The Holy Father makes that so clear. The essential mission of the Church is the task of evangelizing all people.

2

Does this mean that every diocese has to have a missionary spirit? Of course it does. Does this mean that every parish should have a sense of being a missionary organism within the Mystical Body of Christ? Of course it does. Does this mean that every Catholic school, every Catholic institution, every Catholic association must in some way reflect the missionary thrust of the Church? Of course it does. Even more than that, does it mean that every Christian who is truly going to be a Christian in the total, most profound, and most perfect sense of the word must be a missionary, must be an evangelizer, must be a proclaimer of the Good News of Jesus Christ? Of course it does. May I just add one other note here? Does it mean that every seminary should, in a very special way, be preparing its young men for priestly ministry in a missionary context? Of course it does.

Now it is easy for us to say this, but it's sometimes hard for us totally to understand what that fully means in our lives. It means we have to learn how to evangelize. It means we have to be totally committed to the faith that we profess. It means we have to be willing to accept the leadership of the Church, pope, bishops, pastors, and directors of missionary societies, clergy and religious, and laity as well. I always think of Pauline Jaricot, who founded the Society for the Propagation of the Faith, a young lay woman in France in the 19th century. This is role for all of us. It's easy to keep repeating it because it is so absolutely true. We have heard it said by Jesus in the Gospels. We have read it in the great encyclical *Redemptoris Missio* of the present Holy Father, Pope John Paul II. It is the command of the Lord, himself, "Go out into the world, make disciples of every creature" (Mt 28:19; Mk 16:15).²

This was not said to the priests alone, not said to the bishops alone. It was said to everyone who was standing there in front of Jesus on the day of the Ascension, and we are all standing here in front of him now. Just as clearly as we have heard him say: "You shall love the Lord, your God with all your heart and you shall love your neighbor as yourself," so this command to be missionary follows so closely that command of charity, that command of love (Mk 12:20-21). I believe that this is the key and the secret power of all evangelization. If you really love your neighbor, what is the best thing you can give him or her? It is your faith, even more than your life, because faith is the beginning of eternal life and there is nothing more important than that.

As we walk through this earthly pilgrimage, this wonderful journey of our lives, we know that we have to walk it in love, and love is unintelligible, a wise man once told me, except in terms of sacrifice, except in terms of gift-giving. How can you live with somebody you love if you never give them a gift, if you never reach out to them and want to make them happier, make them better, make them more comfortable? How can you live with someone who does not believe in Jesus without wanting every moment of the time to tell them about Jesus? Not just to tell them about Jesus; the Lord doesn't give us that as his command. He says, "Make disciples of them."

Let me tell you a story. Some years ago, shortly after I had been named Archbishop of Newark, I was traveling in India for the Migration and Refugee Services Department of the United States Catholic Conference. During that time, I had the privilege of meeting many of the bishops of India and was very impressed by their wisdom and their zeal. On one such occasion, I was talking to an Indian archbishop and he asked me about my new archdiocese. I was very proud that Newark numbered more than 1.5 million Catholics and so I told him about our Catholic population and how proud I was of the faithful of that local church. I said to him, "Your Grace, how many people do you have?" He answered without any hesitation, "Fifteen million." I said to him, "Oh no, I meant how many Catholics do you have?" And he smiled and replied, "Actually, very few, but aren't we sent to proclaim the Gospel to everybody?" I will never forget that encounter. It was so simple and yet so clear. Aren't we sent to proclaim the Good News to everybody? That is really what it is all about.

And so, to summarize all these words that I've been using. The most perfect gift you can give to somebody else is the faith that you have received freely as a gift from God, the faith that comes to us from the truth of the Gospel, the faith that comes from the grace of the Sacraments, the faith that comes from the Eucharistic presence of the Lord. The Holy Father,

4

Pope John Paul II, in his latest great encyclical, *On The Eucharist*, speaks powerfully of the centrality of the Eucharist and all that must flow from there. This Eucharistic faith is therefore at the center of all the missionary life of the Church, as it is at the center of the Church itself.[3]

"Blessed are you," the Lord said to Thomas, "Because you have seen Me. All the more blessed are those who have not seen and have believed" (Jn 20:29). That's us. That's the Church of the year 2003. There are very few of us who have seen the Lord, although in the holiness of many people today I have no doubt that some have reached that level of contemplation where the Lord is very present to them. But most of us have not seen the Lord. We have not seen him except we do see him in the wonder of the Sacraments. We hear him in the eloquence of the Gospels, we touch him in the courage of martyrdom of so many of our brothers and sisters, even in the world of today.

I remember when I was a young bishop, I think it around the time of the Council of Trent, I was sitting at a November meeting of the bishops' conference, and Archbishop Fulton Sheen was there. As you know, his cause for beatification has just been received in Rome, so we can speak of the Servant of God, Fulton John Sheen. The Archbishop didn't often come to the bishops' meetings in my time. He was retired by the time I became a bishop and he often did not stay for the whole meeting. This one day, he stayed for part of it and as he got up to leave, for some reason or other everybody stopped and watched him. With that wonderful sense of theater that made him so powerful a preacher, he sensed that all our eyes were on him and he went to the microphone. Immediately whoever was presiding said, "Archbishop Sheen, would you like to address the bishops?"

With those great, piercing eyes which never lost their luster or their brilliance, he began to speak of Saint Paul. And with those melodious tones of his, he spoke of Saint Paul at the Areopagus, where Paul decided to preach a more complex homily, a sermon that would capture the philosophy of the Greeks and move it along to a greater understanding of Christian philosophy. Archbishop Sheen's commentary was three words: "And he failed." Paul's sermon was a disaster. His listeners just weren't touched. Paul knew that it was a disaster and he never preached that way again. From then on, Archbishop Sheen continued, Paul went to Corinth, where he stayed for two years. In Corinth, he consistently proclaimed one simple theme: We preach Jesus, crucified, risen, and coming again. What

Paul learned was a great lesson and he taught it to us. Fulton Sheen concluded with the words: "That is what we must preach today and nothing else will ever do." And then he walked away and we all stood up and clapped. It was a wonderful moment because we bishops felt that we had been evangelized, that someone had clearly told us the message of the Gospel. It is the message of the Church, because the Church is an evangelizing Church, and without that we are really nothing. Saint Paul tells us, "I am lost if I do not preach the Gospel" (1 Cor 9:16). So am I. And so are you.

But how do we preach the Gospel? How do we truly be missionaries in today's world? Here there are three points I want to make. First of all, we have to know what the Gospel says. We have to take it and read it and understand it, the Gospel in one hand and the *Catechism of the Catholic Church* (CCC) in the other. We have to appreciate that we cannot just go out and say that "Jesus Christ is Lord." In today's world, we have to know what comes before that and what comes after. We have to know what the Gospel says. We have to know what it means. It is the voice of the Church today and therefore the voice of Christ today.[4]

Secondly, we have to tell it like it is. I think of Saint Paul's criticism of those who do not preach the Gospel correctly, who twist it for their own desires or their own projects. Forgive me for being very direct when I say that there really is no place in evangelization for those who tell us: "I will accept this and not that," the so-called "cafeteria Catholics" of today. The Gospel is one piece. It is one seamless garment. We have to take it all. Jesus is not in pieces. He is one, and he inspires Paul to proclaim: "One Lord, one faith, one baptism, one God and Father of us all" (Eph 4:5-6).

Thirdly, the evangelist must speak from the heart. The evangelist must know what he or she is all about, know what he or she needs to proclaim, the truth of the Gospel, the power of the doctrine, and to build on that a solid foundation of faith. To know what it says and to know what it means ultimately is to let it be alive in us, because if it is not alive in us it is not alive in what we say, in what we proclaim. To know it well, to accept it all, to live it: these are the marks of the true evangelist, I believe.

Let me develop the third element a little more deeply. There is a great story that the present Bishop of Lexington used to tell in retreats. It's a story about the old fathers of the desert, those early hermit monks who went off into the deserts of Egypt during the time of the persecutions and during the time of the laxity of materialism that threatened the Church as it entered the relative peace of the fourth century. The monks would find refuge in the mountains and hills and in the desert places and once in a while young people would come to them to learn how to meditate and to discern the deepest things of God. The hermits tell the story that one of these old desert fathers had a dog and the dog was very energetic. One day while the father was talking to a couple of his younger disciples, the dog was sleeping nearby and a fox appeared on the outreaches. The dog perhaps smelled the fox and immediately woke up, saw the fox, and began to yelp and bark and run after the fox. This began a chase that went on for a long time. Because of the yelping of the dog, other dogs began to follow and soon the chase was joined by at least a dozen dogs.

The fox was very fast and fleet of foot, and also probably very scared, and so he ran and ran and ran as fast as he could. The dogs kept running, but after awhile, little by little, the dogs tired and dropped off until at the end it was only the old hermit's dog that kept running after the fox. Eventually, the chase ended and the fox found his way into a lair that the dog couldn't find, and the dog came back.

Two young disciples had watched the chase with interest and after it ended, they turned to the old hermit monk and asked him, "Why did all the other dogs stop running and only your dog kept going after the fox?" The old man thought for a moment and smiled and he said to them, "My dog was the only one who had really seen the fox. The others saw him running after it and joined in the chase, but the only one who had really seen and known what it was all about was this dog of mine."

Dear sisters and brothers, in the background music of this wonderful story I see Mary Magdalene coming down from the hill of Calvary, coming down from her wondrous visit to the Holy Sepulchre, to the empty tomb, and breaking into the discussions and the lamentations and the fears of the eleven Apostles and saying to them those five extraordinary words, "I have seen the Lord" (Lk 24: 9-11).

Dear sisters and brothers, this is fundamental. We all must build on that. Without it there is nothing. We must have seen the Lord. We must have seen him in the Gospels. We must have seen him in the Sacraments. We must have seen him in the gathering of the people at Mass, in the ecclesia of God. We must have seen him in the faces of God's wonderful good people. But once we have seen him, once we know the wonder, the beauty, the glory of his Presence in our world, we can't keep it to ourselves, and that's what it means to be a missionary.

Are there problems in being a missionary? Of course there are. Let's talk about some of them. First of all, there are cultural problems. There are problems related to the moment in which we live. Once again, let's go back to *Evangelii Nuntiandi* of Pope Paul VI:

> Evangelization loses much of its force and effectiveness if it does not take into consideration the actual people to whom it is addressed, if it does not use their language, their signs and symbols, if it does not answer the questions they ask, and if it does not have an impact on their concrete life. (EN, no. 63)

How important it is for us to understand the problems of culture, how carefully Pope Paul VI singles out the areas of which we must be aware as we try to proclaim the Gospel to people, to the actual people to whom it is to be addressed! You've got to be there with them. You've got to understand them. You've got to see their hopes, their dreams, their sorrows, their problems, their joys, what makes them laugh, and what makes them cry. You have to use their language, you have to use their signs and their symbols. What a beautiful thought! You have to answer the questions they ask, and not everyone asks the same questions.

I just returned from a couple of visits to Central Asia. I was in Iran for a few days' visit just recently. I hope I have learned how important it is to listen to the questions people ask: questions about God, questions about holiness. Many people have never heard of Jesus. Many of them yearn for a sense of God, yearn for holiness, yearn for an answer to the mysteries of their lives. We have that answer in the mystery of Jesus Christ: mystery for

mystery, love for love, Good News for the world. In Sudan I saw starvation and misery and the terrible plight of families who, in order to save most of their children, had come to the terrible realization that they must sell one or two of them into slavery. I don't know how you make that decision, but I've seen the desperation in the eyes of people who have made it and the resignation in the eyes of young people who have had it made for them. They need the Gospel to be translated into their culture but not to be distorted. It is still the Gospel of Jesus. It is still the Gospel of the God who loves us, and the God who proclaims that heaven and earth are passing away and only his love remains.

I sat on the floor of an ancient house with one of the great Grand Ayatollahs of Shiite Islam, and talked about the things of God. All the great things that the Ayatollah said, and all the reverence that he had, not just for the prophet Mohammed, but also for the prophet Abraham and the prophet Jesus were glorious to listen to, and I said to myself, "Go one step further. See in Jesus Christ the only name in which everything is solved, the only sacrifice by which everyone is saved." And so there are cultural problems.

Secondly, there are social problems. There are people who are so poor that you cannot preach to them right away. There are people who are so brainwashed that you cannot get to them, get to their inner senses right away. There are people who are so distracted with the things of this world that they have put off indefinitely any contemplation of the world to come, until maybe it is too late to see that world as it really is. For all of these, we can unfold the treasures of our Catholic social teaching. It does have answers for the many problems of our society and it has guidelines to help our sisters and brothers in other economic and political systems to find a way out of the turmoil and complexity of the modern and post-modern world. It even has answers for us as we seek to make sense of our increasingly interdependent society and find a way to create globalization with a conscience.

Thirdly, there are methodological problems. There are two extremes in missionary activity. On the one hand, the excesses of the Crusades, and on the other hand, the excesses of the proselytizing of the so-called Rice Christians. In both instances, much is, in principle, understandable. There is good will mixed up in the context of the missionaries' own time and own culture. In the Muslim world, the word "crusade" evokes a very hostile message; and not just in the Muslim world, but in so much of the world of Orthodox Christians. Remember that the Crusades, which started out with the blessing of the popes to win back the Holy Land as a place of pilgrimage and peaceful Christian presence, and which brought many holy people to its support, soon became mixed up in the political and military and economic competition of the early nation-states and ended up doing much harm to many people.

This is the one extreme example of an incomplete methodology of missionary activity. It arises when we lose sight of the essence of evangelization, which must always be based on charity and never on an overbearing arrogance or a lack of respect for the dignity of those to whom we are sent. The opposite extreme is the case of the Rice Christians. This was an attempt to buy the hearts and minds of others. It sometimes surfaces also when the evangelist teaches the faith to fit what he or she thinks will please the prospective hearers. This also is not just an offense against the dignity of our teaching, but a disdain for the dignity of those who receive the watered-down doctrine.

The fourth danger in the missionary life is what we could call its completeness. I spoke of it moments ago when I spoke of teaching the faith to fit the moment, picking and choosing what you think others want to hear. One of the great crises of missionary life today, especially in some parts of the Orient, is our need to proclaim Jesus not simply as a good man, not simply as a great teacher, not even simply as a wonderful prophet, but as the Son of the Living God. We dare not misinterpret the Gospel or the teaching of the Church or the last case will be worse than the first.

Another common problem, which all of us who have any administrative responsibilities know so well, is the problem of competition: competition for resources, competition for personnel, competition for opportunities. This is the fifth hurdle we must overcome. We are haunted by the limitations of our resources, and opportunities are therefore also limited. We seem to be without the personnel that we had before, without the opportunities we had before, without the extraordinary resources that we had before, even though, thank God, our people remain as generous as they ever were.

It is terrible when the missionary aspect of the life of the Church has to take a back seat because of other apostolates within the Church and yet, as a bishop, I know that this can happen, even sometimes through my own fault and shortsightedness. Education, for example, is such a tremendous need in the Church today and oftentimes education requires so great a share of our budgets. But education must be evangelical too. Isn't it also an evangelizing tool that God has given us? It truly ought to be, and if it is not we must make it so. We must find in every Catholic school in the United States an opportunity to talk about God, to talk about Jesus Christ, to tell the people who we are. Parents who are not Catholic are entrusting their children to us, not to be subtly converted, that's not what it's about, but they must learn who we are. They must learn that in every Catholic church this is what the liturgy is like. In every Catholic school this is what is taught. You don't have to believe it if you don't have the gift of our Catholic faith, but you should know what we are all about. We should not treat it as something hidden, or of which we are ashamed, but exalt in joy about our faith so it will be catching.

Let me talk to you for a moment about a bad mistake in pastoral theology that comes from that fifth danger. Years ago, pastors would come to bishops (I know by actual experience), and say, "Let me close my school and then I'll have time for evangelization. The school takes all my money, takes all my time." And you would visit that parish in the morning or go for a meeting there, and here the pastor would be, outside, complaining about the school. And you would see 800 youngsters, Catholic and non-Catholic, milling around, playing, waiting for the bell to ring, waiting to go

*"It is a task and mission which the vast and profound changes of present-day society make all the more urgent. Evangelizing is in fact the grace and vocation proper to the Church, her deepest identity. She exists to evangelize."*

(EN, no.14)

in and start their school day. And the pastor would come up to me and say, "Bishop, I just can't wait until I get rid of this school and can start really evangelizing." And here in the school are 800 souls waiting to hear the Good News of Jesus Christ, and maybe 400 families to which they belong. Are you going to close your school and lose all these potential apostles, or most of them? And then are you really going to evangelize? What a chance to do it now! What a chance to do it when all your people are at home in your parish school, in your church, in your facilities. A parish with a school is a tremendous tool of evangelization. What a disaster ever to lose it.

Dear sisters and brothers, we have to recognize these dangers and face them squarely and with courage and vision. We cannot let ourselves be overcome by the immensity of the world's problems. The world has always had its problems and they are always too much for us to handle. But the world, as we know it, is passing away. Do not give in to that overwhelming feeling that we cannot possibly solve all the problems. By ourselves we cannot, but listen to the words of the ancient Scriptures: "The zeal for Thy House, O Lord, has eaten me up" (Ps 69:10)! This is what they sang in a church of one of our minority communities that I was in last week: "The zeal for your house has consumed me." And that's the great zeal that we need in educating people and challenging people and calling people to holiness, in proclaiming boldly the message that Jesus Christ is Lord!

Dear sisters and brothers, how can I summarize this message of evangelization that I want to leave with you this evening? I need to go back to something I said at the beginning of this talk. Deep in my heart, I believe that evangelization is intimately related to charity. If we are unkind, if we are arrogant, then we will never, ever find open hearts or open minds. We will never inspire anyone to become a disciple of the Lord because it will not be the Good News that we are proclaiming, but ourselves, and that is not where grace is. There is a challenge in our Church for the bishop, for the parish priest, for the hermit, for the solitary monk, for the religious sister and brother, for the lay teacher and the catechist, for the young and the old, the sick and the hale. There is room for all of us and a challenge for each of us. We must evangelize. Forgive me the secular language, but in the worldly vocabulary of our century, we must market this wondrous gift of Jesus Christ to the world.

We are ambassadors for Christ, the Scriptures tell us. We are the chosen salespeople of Christ, too. It is maybe a less lofty occupation, but it is much needed in today's world. And just as kindness and courtesy are always the keys to marketing success, so kindness is always the great key to evangelization. Do you buy from a cranky sales person? Do you tip a cranky waiter? We don't need Rice Christians anymore; if you'll forgive me, what we need are nice Christians. We will always need nice Christians. The story of the early Church is still with us. The voices of our neighbors, even though they knew the difficulties and persecutions that haunted the Christians' lives, were constantly saying, "See those Christians, how they love one another." We must still be able to say that today. That is one of the secrets of evangelization.

We will never be able to afford these mega-churches with fluorescent lights and mighty megaphones that blare and blast. We will probably never have multi-million-dollar organs on every floor of wondrous buildings built with gold. I pray that God will be worshipped in those buildings, and I have hope that he is. But our road is the road of Jesus and we know that we cannot proclaim his Good News well without the gold of kindness and the precious jewel of honesty. We will never reach out to our neighbors unless we are loving and patient and kind. We will never make a difference in the world unless we are generous and forgiving, unless we know who we are and what our Lord has called us to be.

The universal language of the Gospel is the language of faith and love and even that faith must be formed by the great virtue of charity. This is the key to evangelization as well as the answer to all that we need in our

families and in our homes and in our lives. The foundation for our happiness in this life will come from a realization of our burning need to evangelize: not just to talk about Jesus to other people, but to model his teaching in such a way that they become disciples, not hearers of the Word, but doers also. Once again, listen to the voice of the teaching Church. I cite *Go and Make Disciples*, the 1992 statement by the bishops of the United States: "The fruits of evangelization are changed lives and a changed world."[5]

In a wonderful way, that completes the circle. The Good News of Jesus can only be proclaimed through kindness and love, and once it has been proclaimed, it becomes the seed and the sowing and indeed the harvest that changes and redeems the world. Let it be even so for us and for all who believe that Jesus Christ is Lord.

1   Pope Paul VI, *Evangelii Nuntiandi: On Evangelization in the Modern World* (Washington, DC: USCCB, 1975 ).
2   Pope John Paul II, *Redemptoris Missio: On The Permanent Validity Of The Church's Missionary Mandate* (Washington, DC: USCCB, 1990).
3   Pope John Paul II, *Ecclesia de Eucharistia: On the Eucharist* (Washington, DC: USCCB, 2003).
4   *Catechism of the Catholic Church*, 2nd ed. (Washington, DC: USCCB, 1997).
5   United States Conference of Catholic Bishops, *Go and Make Disciples* (Washington, DC: USCCB, 2002),11, Sec. 18.

# REFLECTION QUESTIONS

Preaching the Gospel means that we must know what it says, preach it in its entirety, and live it so that we can speak it from our hearts. Reflect on your own experience. With which of these points are you most comfortable and why? In which area(s) are you challenged to grow? How might you do this?

Reflect on the five challenges that we can face in our efforts to evangelize: cultural problems, social problems, methodological problems, completeness in presenting the Gospel, and competition within church structures. Which one(s) present the greatest challenge to you and how might you begin to address that challenge?

Cardinal McCarrick says that "evangelization is intimately related to charity." When have you experienced this from others? When have others experienced this from you? Discuss some "evangelizing moments" when the practice of charity might be most needed.

---

**His Eminence Theodore Cardinal McCarrick** *is Archbishop of Washington, D.C. A native of New York City, he was ordained to the priesthood by Cardinal Spellman in 1958 and earned his Ph.D. from Catholic University. In 1965, he was named president of the Catholic University of Puerto Rico in Ponce. In 1969 he returned to New York and was ordained auxiliary bishop of New York in 1977. In 1981 he was appointed the first bishop of Metuchen, New Jersey, and in 1986 he was appointed archbishop of Newark, a position he held until his appointment as the archbishop of Washington. He was installed in Washington in January of 2001 and was elevated to the College of Cardinals seven weeks later on February 21. He has served as chair of the USCCB committees on Migration, Aid to the Church in Central and Eastern Europe, and International Policy. In addition to serving on several USCCB committees, he is currently the chancellor of the Catholic University of America and chairman of the board of trustees of the Basilica of the National Shrine of the Immaculate Conception. He also serves on the board of directors of Catholic Relief Services and is a member of the Pontifical Council for Justice and Peace.*

# General Session

## EVANGELIZATION AND NORTH AMERICAN CULTURE

Eric H. F. Law

After four months of exploration and reflection on why they were not able to grow, members of a shrinking, aging congregation arrived at the following action plan: they took out the last two pews in the back of the church and set up a quiet play area for children. When newcomers with young children came to church, they could leave their children right there and worship in the church, knowing their children would be near them and safe. The congregation's goal was to become a church that welcomed families with children, and by doing that, they hoped to increase their membership by 15 percent in six months. Within a month, nineteen new children and their parents were coming to church consistently. The church had exceeded its modest goal in a fraction of the time set forth in the action plan. Word of this success traveled quickly to other parts of the denomination.

A group of leaders in another church heard about this success story and decided that they would implement the same idea. They said, "We are in the exact same situation that this church was in—an aging congregation, unable to attract younger newcomers with children. If this idea works for them, then it should work for us. It's simple enough to do." When the leaders removed the last two pews, the whole congregation was up in arms about it. People complained that they were not consulted on this change. They grumbled, "Without those last two pews,

17

the church just isn't the same. And by the way, what happened to the little brass memorial plates on the sides of these pews?" Of course, then there were children in the play area, and the parishioners complained about the noise and the bad behavior of the children. Within a month, the church had restored everything back to the way it was. This congregation did not gain any new young families with children.

Why did this technique work well in one place and not in another? The idea worked for the first congregation because there was a change in the fundamental perception of the church members about themselves and the community around them. In four months spent reflecting on their issues, they had moved the congregation from operating out of a maintenance model to a missionary model of church.[1]

The external change was accompanied by an internal transformation. This kind of internal change has been called many different names by many writers on organizational change: transformational change, adaptive change, reorientation, recreation, discontinuous change, organizational culture change, paradigm shift, deep change, and profound change. They all point to a deeper internal change that accompanies the external change of behavior, structure and system.

Alan Roxburgh in his book *Crossing the Bridge* said that this kind of transition is not a linear one, through which we try to move our church community from one set of behaviors and structures to another. "It is about reconnecting with the core story and tradition so that they are freed from the old frameworks. When this happens, there is freedom to recognize the values and frameworks that must be released so that our systems can move toward the reinventing of a missional future."[2]

In order to accomplish this profound change, the first step is to find a way to discover the old frameworks, assumptions, and patterns that are no longer appropriate or relevant in responding to the challenges and changes around us. Since these frameworks, assumptions, and patterns have developed over a long period of time, much of the development might be unconscious to most church members. The crucial step to our change model is to reveal these mostly unconscious, unspoken assumptions. Once we can see and articulate them, we can then entertain the possibility of changing them.

Many church leaders have come to me time and time again and reported that the moment they realized their church could change was the moment when the church members could finally discuss the "unspeakable." To help readers understand what this step involves, I will again utilize the "iceberg analogy." This is an image I used in my first book, *The Wolf Shall Dwell with the Lamb,* to help people understand intercultural conflicts. The following is an expanded description of this analogy, applying it to organization change.[3]

An iceberg has a small piece above the water that we can easily see, and a much larger irregular piece submerged under the water that we cannot see, nor do we know is even there. Throughout history, the submerged parts of icebergs have  been responsible for many shipwrecks, precisely because we could not see them. The part above the water represents the external culture and the part under the water represents the internal cultural of an organization. Profound change happens not with the external culture of the organization; it must occur from a transformation of the internal culture. Let us apply this analogy to our church organization, starting with the external culture of the Church.

In the organizational culture of the church, the part above the water— the external culture—includes the appearance of the physical buildings of the church, our worship proceedings, our music, our doctrine, our explicit organizational structure and decision-making process, our stated mission, etc. These are the things that we can see, hear, taste, and touch. We are conscious of their existence. We can readily articulate why they are there. A purely external cultural element of an organization is very easily changed to adapt to something new. Usually these are changes that do not require shifting the core assumptions, frameworks, and patterns of the organization. In other words, the kind of adjustments at this level do not require a profound change. For example, the old water fountain located by the bathroom of a church broke down. The building and grounds committee met and decided to replace the

**Figure 4.1 Iceberg Analogy of Organization Culture**

**EXTERNAL CULTURE**

Explicit organization structure, policies and decision-making process, physical buildings, worship proceedings

- Conscious
- Easily Changed
- Objective Knowledge

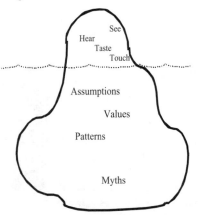

**INTERNAL CULTURE**

Implicit decision-making process, assumed framework, informal leaders, unarticulated beliefs and values

- Unconscious
- Difficult to Change
- Subjective Knowledge

fountain with a freestanding water dispenser from a distilled water company that would deliver water every week. In the meeting, committee members arrived at this decision for the following reasons:

1. The tap water coming out of the fountain was full of minerals and it did not taste very good.

2. The fountain broke down because of the mineral build-up from the unfiltered water.

The committee members also considered whether they could afford the new water dispenser with the ongoing cost of water delivery and the cost of paper cups. They checked the budget, and yes, they could afford it. They voted on it and added the item into the budget permanently. In a week, the dispenser was in place and everyone appreciated it.

This is purely an external cultural change and the reasons behind the decision were very clear. The committee was dealing with something it could see and taste and touch. The objective was clear, and the group consciously made the decision and changed it.

Many authors on change models refer to this purely external cultural change as technical change, surface change, or incremental change. It is technical because it requires only the changing of the physical arrangement of things. It does not require any change of the deeper core assumptions of the church. It is incremental because the added budget item constitutes a small addition to the overall structure of the budget, and does not require a shift in paradigm in people's perception of the church. This change does not challenge the deeply held assumptions, frameworks, patterns, and myths of the community.

But, as most of us who have attempted to implement it in the church know, change often involves more than just the physical environment or people's behavior. For example, if the water fountain had been donated by a very prominent member of the church, the change described above might not have been simple. If there was a myth deep in the organizational iceberg attached to this objective, replacing it would have required more than just an explicit rational discussion. More often than not, when we move something that seems like a purely external cultural element, we encounter major inertia. It feels like we are dragging a lot of things that we cannot even name.

I was invited to consult with a church that was struggling with what it called the "kitchen" problem. The complaint initially came from the people who worshipped at the 9:00 a.m. English-speaking service.

"The Korean congregation at 11:00 comes into the kitchen way too early," they griped. "We almost never get to use the kitchen to prepare for our coffee hour."

I asked them, "What have you done to address this problem?"

They said they had put up a schedule on the kitchen wall stating very clearly that from 8:30 to 10:30 a.m., the kitchen was to be used by the English-speaking congregation only, and from 10:30 a.m. to 1:00 p.m., the kitchen was to be used by the Korean congregation. They seemed to be addressing this problem purely from an external cultural level at this point. I asked them if the schedule worked to solve their problem.

"It kind of worked for a while, but now we are hearing complaints about who stinks up the kitchen with what smell."

As I suspected, the problem had transformed itself into something else. So, I asked them what they had done this time to address the new complaint.

"We put up another sign and we bought a large can of odor neutralizer. The sign says, 'SPRAY BEFORE YOU GO.'"

"Did that work?" I asked.

"Not really. Now we are hearing complaints about the Korean children running around the parish hall and kitchen, and making too much noise."

When we address a seemingly external problem by using an external solution and the problem does not go away, then we are dealing with more than just the external culture. We must look at the internal culture, the part of the organization's iceberg that is below the water.

The real issue from the above example was that in the submerged part, two very different icebergs were bumping against each other. The presence of the growing Korean congregation posed a major challenge to the assumed framework, pattern, and myths of the English-speaking congregation. The complaints about the kitchen were just the surface expression of this unconscious challenge.

Let me offer another example. In the 1960s, we observed people in the South being segregated—that is, people of difference races were not mixing. If we had simply treated that as an external cultural issue, an external cultural solution would have been to physically mix people of different races together. The most well-known approach of this kind was "busing." We bused people of different races to one place and forced them to mix together in one classroom. But that did not solve our problem of segregation. Instead, the people who were forced together did not get along. There were tensions, conflicts, and even physical violence.

But we still thought that was only an external cultural problem. So we implemented another external solution. When people fought, we sent in law enforcement to stop them from fighting. This did not solve the problem, it only complicated it some more. The real issue was that the cultural icebergs of the different racial groups were colliding under the water. Both groups challenged each other's assumptions, patterns, myths, and cultural

frameworks at the unconscious level. If we were going to move both groups toward constructive change, we would have to address the issue from that deeper, profound level. Profound change has to come from exploring the internal part of our cultural icebergs.

The internal culture is the larger irregular part below the water level of our cultural iceberg. These are beliefs and values that we have implicitly learned. They are unconscious to us and therefore very difficult to change. They are patterns in our lives that we have accepted as normal. They consist of myths—stories that we learned when we were young like fairy tales—or events and stories from past generations that have, over time, sunk to the bottom of our cultural iceberg.

Even though these myths and patterns are unconscious to us, they still condition the way we perceive and react to the world around us. They are subjective knowledge. They are there, but we cannot explain them. For example, a child asks, "Why do we do it this way?" Many of us might find ourselves saying something like, "Because I said so," or simply "Because!" This is not something objective that we teach our children. We are teaching them something subjective, a pattern with no explanation, an unspoken value or belief that is unconscious.

Let me illustrate the connection between the external and internal culture by using another example from education. A teacher says to a class, "Your class participation counts a lot for your final grade." This is the external part of what is taught—we can hear the teacher say it, we are conscious of this saying, and perhaps even believe that it is objective. But let us examine what this statement might teach us implicitly in our internal culture in the United States.

*"Culture is the special way in which human beings express and develop their relationship with creation, with one another and with God. . . . The Church, which accompanies human beings on life's path, opening to the life of society, seeking opportunities for her evangelizing action, embraces culture in her word and action."*

John Paul II
Speech at the University of Havana (January 23, 1998), no. 2

When we say "class participation," we usually mean speaking on behalf of oneself. This is not a universal concept. In Hong Kong, where I grew up, we were given a grade for class participation also. However, our class participation was measured by how well we did not stand out from the group with which we were working. This was a very different concept of participation, shaping a very different internal cultural iceberg for the students in Hong Kong.

Let us come back to the internal cultural iceberg of the United States, where participation means speaking on behalf of oneself. If a class is one hour long and has thirty students, equal participation of everyone would mean each student has two minutes to participate. But that rarely happens, because the teacher usually speaks for about forty-five minutes in most of the classes I have attended. If the teacher speaks for forty-five minutes, we only have fifteen minutes left for thirty students to participate.

In the United States, we profess on the external cultural level that all people are equal. So if everyone is equal, each student can only have thirty seconds to participate. But that is physically impossible, because if a student talks and the teacher responds, that exchange usually takes up two minutes, so that with the remaining fifteen minutes, only seven or eight students out of thirty can really participate. What might this be teaching our students implicitly and unconsciously?

When I described the above scenario in a workshop and posted the same question, participants eventually arrived at the conclusion that we are teaching our students "competition for time." Not only are we teaching them competition, we are teaching them a particular concept of time. Time is a commodity; if they are to do well in this class, they have to claim their share of time. They have learned that time is worth a lot to their grade. Later, when our children grow up, they might say, "Time is money" as if it were a normal assumption for everyone.

Now imagine an immigrant family with a young child from a cultural environment that does not teach such competition, entering our school system for the first time? After only one day of school, the child returns home and starts demanding time from her parents. Her parents ask, "Why are you so rude today? What did you learn in school?" The little child says, "I learned the letters A, B, and C. I learned to add and subtract. I played computer games and met a lot of new friends."

She cannot tell her parents that she learned how to compete for time, because she did not learn it explicitly.

I would think none of us have ever heard a teacher in the United States says to a class in this way, "If you want to get an A, you have to learn to compete for time." We have never heard it, but we all learned it nonetheless. Competition for time is whispered through almost every classroom in the United States. There might be exceptions in which a teacher consciously decides not to teach competition and creates a cooperative learning environment. But the moment the students leave that classroom and move on to another classroom, "competition for time" is taught again and again, unconsciously and implicitly.

We bring these internal cultural elements unconsciously into our church. Collectively, we create the internal organizational culture of our church.

Let us now look specifically at the internal organizational culture of a church—the part of the iceberg that is submerged below the waterline and cannot be seen. These are the assumptions, values, patterns, and myths

25

that are implicitly imbedded in an organization, often unconscious to its members, but are key to the identity and operation of the community.

 Using the above example, a church in which most of its members were educated in the United States might believe with all their hearts that they should be inclusive of a particular ethnic group that had immigrated and settled in their neighborhood. In their effort to include the immigrants, the members invited them to come to a meeting so that they could explore ways to meet each other's needs in the community. During the meeting, the church members assumed unconsciously that everyone knew how to compete for time and therefore spoke freely about what was on their minds. As the meeting proceeded, the members became more and more frustrated because their guests did not say anything or offer any suggestions. The meeting was a "waste of time" to them. Here, with all good intentions and even a great plan, but without the awareness of the immigrants' internal culture, the members were not able to realize their goal.

The internal culture includes the unconscious patterns that the community repeats over and over again. When confronted with the question of why a community maintains a pattern, the reply is often, "We have always done it that way." There are implicit decision-making processes and unspoken rules based on values that are so deeply held that no one has articulated them for a long time.

These processes also involve informal leaders of the church. These are people who have no formal leadership roles; they are not on any committees, but they seem to have a lot of influence in the decision-making of the church.

The internal culture of a church also includes myths by which the community lives. Myths are stories that the community knew in the past, but over time and generations have become unconscious to most members. These myths might revolve around particular personalities in the past, or traumatic experiences that were not dealt with constructively or worked through by the community. These myths might create an unconscious pattern that the church community keeps repeating and is not able to be free of, until the myths become conscious again. Since these myths are unconscious, they are very hard to change. How do you change something that you don't know exists?

When we talk about evangelization, especially of a different cultural group from ourselves and our church community, we are dealing with the bumping of two or more different cultural icebergs. The bumping often happens on the internal, under-the-water level. We might not know why the others are not receiving or welcoming our goodwill or services.

In the old days, for example, many European Christian missionaries put a cross on top of their cultural iceberg: sometimes they were not able to acknowledge the difference between their cultural values and beliefs, and the Gospel. In fact, many of the missionaries thought the two were the same.

With all good intentions and passion for the Good News, these missionaries traveled to different communities to spread the Gospel as they understood it. When they encountered another group from a different cultural iceberg, they were actually bumping into each other on the internal level.

On the surface, the groups might still have been at a very "safe" distance; one group did not understand why the other did not want to get any closer.

Some of the missionaries who did not understand this dynamic got very frustrated. They might have asked, "Why don't they like us? We are good, friendly, and kind Christian folks. Why don't they like the good news of Jesus Christ that we are trying to proclaim?"

With that, the missionaries might have pushed the others a little, and with the iceberg conflict below the water, the natives might have retreated or even gotten defensive. What the missionaries did not understand was that the natives were resisting the internal unconscious cultural framework that the newcomers brought with them, not the Gospel. Encountering resistance, some European missionaries might have concluded that there was something "wrong" with the others' culture. So the missionaries may have pushed even harder, crushing the others' iceberg in order to reshape it into looking like their own.

For example, when I worked in a Chinese church, I noticed that Chinese Christian communities often sang hymns with a European tune and Chinese lyrics forced into the melody. Whoever translated the hymn did not have a full understanding of the tonality and rhythm of the Chinese language. For example, the word for "Lord" in Cantonese sounds like "jeu" said in a lower tone from the throat. The word for "pig" has the same sound "jeu" but said in a higher tone from the nose. Musically, the two words are about four notes apart. If the translator of the hymn did not understand this and placed the word "Lord" at a higher note, "O Lord have mercy" might be sung as, "O Pig have mercy." To this day, there are hymns that the Chinese community refuses to sing because they sound like swearing.

Since I was a composer, I decided to write some new hymns using a text from the Psalms, paying special attention to the tonality of the Chinese language. When I finished, I chose a melody that sounded like a traditional Chinese folk tune: it used a five-note (pentatonic) scale. I gave the hymn to the choir and the choir was nice enough to sing it, perhaps out of respect for me as a priest. After they performed, one of the choir members came to me and asked, "Fr. Law, how come your hymn sounds so Buddhist?"[4]

This incident caused me to reflect on what happened to the Chinese community when the Gospel was transmitted to it by the European missionaries. In effect, a chunk of the Chinese cultural iceberg was thrown out and replaced with the adage that "a hymn is not a hymn unless it sounds European."

This example illustrates the importance of knowing one's internal cultural iceberg in the work of evangelization. The first step to becoming an interculturally sensitive evangelist is to know one's iceberg—having the discipline to consciously differentiate between one's internal cultural values, myths, and patterns, and the Gospel's values and patterns. If we have limited knowledge of our cultural iceberg and are not careful when we encounter others, we might be in danger of crushing the other's iceberg.

1   For a detailed comparison of maintenance and missionary models, see Claude E. Payne and Hamilton Beazley, *Reclaiming the Great Commission* (San Francisco: Jossey-Bass, 2000), 48–49.
2   Alan Roxburgh, *Crossing the Bridge* (Costa Mesa, CA: Percept Group, Inc., 2000), 61.
3   Eric H. F. Law, *The Wolf Shall Dwell With the Lamb* (St. Louis: Chalice Press, 1993), 4–10.
4   Eric H. F. Law, *Sacred Acts, Holy Change: Faithful Diversity and Practical Transformation* (Chalice Press: St. Louis, 2002), 33–46.

# REFLECTION QUESTIONS

Given what has happened since September 11, 2001, what "iceberg pieces" have been exposed within yourself and your community?

Consider assumptions, values, fears, patterns, beliefs, myths, etc. What are the values, assumptions, patterns, beliefs, and myths of your generation that influence the way you treat others who may or may not be in your age group?

Eric Law states that in order for a congregation to move out of a maintenance model to a missionary model the fundamental perception of church must change. Brainstorm components that keep your community in a maintenance model. Discuss, for these may challenge you to change and move towards a missionary model.

---

**Eric H.F. Law** *is a consultant and trainer in multicultural organization development and building inclusive community—helping educational, health care, and religious institutions constructively address issues of racism and diversity for over ten years. He is the author of several books and publications, and has taught at various institutions around the country. Eric was educated at Cornell University and Episcopal Divinity School and is a priest for the Episcopal Diocese of Los Angeles.*

# General Session

## CREATING A MEDIA LENS FOR EVANGELIZATION

Angela Ann Zukowski, MHSH, D.Min

## The Reality

**M**any of us in ministry may have experienced what I call a Rip Van Winkle Syndrome within the past fifteen years. As you may recall, Rip Van Winkle fell asleep and when he awoke the world had dramatically changed. He meandered around the village trying to make sense of what happened. Where were the familiar people, places and sites that gave him a sense of focus and stability in his life? It had all changed.

You may remember a day when you became conscious (awake) to the reality that something was different in the culture. In particular, something had shifted in how people were communicating and networking together. New advanced communication tools were not only in businesses, but implanted in homes and schools. We discovered that the language being used to communicate had new words, concepts, symbols, and required new skills. How did this happen  without our consent, interest, or concern? Why wasn't our consciousness tickled earlier in our ministry formation to the growing cultural phenomenon?

A few years ago an educational journal exhibited an image of a ten-year-old boy fully equipped to participate in the new communication cultural phenomenon. My first intuition was to perceive this young man as coming from another planet. He displayed a virtual headset and arm wear—

new tools to navigate through a new space called virtual reality. Hanging from the side of his belt was a Palm Pilot along with DVD hardware and software. This was complemented by an over-the-shoulder laptop computer, looking like a small notepad with all the necessary accessories to journey further into another new space called cyberspace. This young man was fully equipped for a multimedia interactive high intensive encounter with the world through communications technology. He was referred to as a "cyberzen" (a citizen of cyberspace).

The accompanying article confirmed that this young man understood the rapidly evolving new culture and had no fear to traverse its frontiers. The image may be daunting but it is the reality we live today. With or without us, this new communication culture is destined to continue to evolve. We need to be alert, understanding, and skilled in this new communication culture if the Gospel message and our new evangelization efforts are to be effectively communicated to future generations.

In the United States, we live in the most sophisticated growing communication culture in history. Where are we as church ministers and leaders? Few of the new ideas about learning or communicating in the communications age have been adequately or widely adopted in the formation of clergy and lay ministry leaders (evangelizers), or in our Catholic colleges and universities, particularly in the fields of theology, pastoral theology, religious studies, and religious education. This has been documented in more than one study in various parts of the world. A few years ago there was one bright light when the Lilly Endowment, in collaboration with Wabash College, offered grants to an ecumenical mix of colleges, universities, and seminaries to explore ways to advance the quality of teaching through multimedia support. These academic institutions are doing interesting research and applications to hone their media/communication skills and to advance the communication technical infrastructure of their institutions.

The journey into the frontiers of a new evangelization is fraught with unknowns. This is the reality of new frontiers. Frequently, barriers are given for not pursuing a radical new pathway. We feel more secure in the familiar and tangible means for measuring our evangelization efforts.

While this is valid, we must move beyond an either/or approach to one that is both/and. We can continue our traditional ways of evangelizing while opening ourselves to new possibilities.

# Expanding Our Avenues for Evangelization

In *The Language of Faith*, Edward Schilleebeckx states, "The Gospel's message is too rich to be contained within one paradigm."[1] There can be no truer words today. We have available to us a kaleidoscope of opportunities and techniques that can be engaged to trigger the religious imagination of women, men, and children alike. In *Communio et Progressio: On the Means of Social Communication* (CP) we read, "The people of God walk in history. As they advance with their times they look forward with confidence and even with enthusiasm to whatever the development of communications in the space age may offer."[2]

*Redemptoris Missio: On the Permanent Validity of the Church's Missionary Mandate* and *Aetatis Nova: On Social Communications on the Twentieth Anniversary of Communio et Progressio*, in calling the Church's attention to her mission indicates that the Church cannot avoid the reality that we are living in a new era rooted in a "'new culture' created by modern communications. . . with new languages, new techniques and a new psychology."[3] By reflecting upon and actualizing the Church's imaginative energies, we can strive to create new methods and expressions for evangelization. We need to be brave, bold, and imaginative!

I teach and work with university students every day. I am challenged to create an environment that can address religious issues and concerns. This is no easy task. When all is said and done, it is more than technique that inspires great questions and conversations. It is who each of us "is" and "becoming" in relationship to the Gospel that inspires an individual to embrace the Faith. This idea is the launching pad for exploring new evangelization opportunities or methods.

# Advent People Open New Doors

The *General Directory for Catechesis* uses the biblical metaphor of the sower who went out to sow the seed when speaking about our mission for proclaiming the Good News amidst a rapidly unfolding new religious panorama.[4] The new religious panorama offers the Church a complexity of challenges for the new millennium. We stand amid a cacophony of images, words, symbols, and sounds that are communicated through a diversity of media. A new era has dawned!

*"Our century is characterized by the mass media or means of social communication, and the first proclamation, catechesis or the further deepening of faith cannot do without these means. . . . When they are put at the service of the Gospel, they are capable of increasing almost indefinitely the area in which the Word of God is heard; they enable the Good News to reach millions of people."*

Pope Paul VI, *Evangelii Nuntiandi: On Evangelization in the Modern World* (Washington, DC: USCCB, 1975), no. 14

The new religious panorama reminds us that we truly are an *Advent* people. We realize that while God's offer already has been revealed in the world, it is yet to be fully received, understood, and accepted. Thus, Advent people open new doors, radiating optimism and possibilities beyond the present situation.

In reflecting on the idea of Advent, Karl Rahner invites us to keep focused on the reality that we are to "cooperatively enact the one and final movement of the world and history toward God's arrival—in freedom, in faith, hope and love." He goes on to say that witnessing is not to the past but to the future. We are a "people of expectation and hope." In a world captivated by the "sense of present time," consumerism, success, and individualism, Advent people must ask themselves "if the spirit and heart in us still have a little room for novelty and future beyond the present."[5]

As with Schilleebeckx, there is an appreciation for diversity, newness, and alternative dimensions for proclaiming the Gospel within contemporary culture. The process begins when an individual is exposed to a life of contemplation and awareness. Rahner indicates that the proclaimer—the sower—must allow time to be silent amid the tumult of the new marketplace.

Only one who can be still and pray, who is patient and does not drown out the frightening silence—in which God dwells and which often comes over us with the racket of everyday life and the shouts of the amusement park of the world—can already hear with ease and appreciate something of the eternal life that is inwardly given to us in this fragmenting time.

The contemplative presence, which fertilizes a connectedness with God, offers individuals revelatory moments for discerning ways to express and position the "hidden energy of the Good News." It is necessary for the Church to continually identify opportunities to break open the Good News through word, image, story, and song, to stimulate the religious imagination of the hearers to desire to respond and say, "Amen" (Rahner, 10).

## The Shifting Panorama

Spiritual seekers, fundamentalism, secularism, new age spiritualities, faith syncretism, and the increase in Muslims, Hindus, Christ Clubs, Pentecostals, and Evangelicals signal that the Church needs to rethink her paradigms for "positioning" or "imagining" the Good News of Jesus in this exploding religious panorama. As each of these religious groups amplifies their beliefs via radio, television, music, print, and in cyberspace, the Church cannot allow her own belief system and understanding of the Gospel to be silent, distorted, or distant from the expanding media milieu.

The assent to particular doctrines, creeds, teachings, and religious commitments in recent centuries has become problematic for many. We find ourselves in a new religious spiritual context that did not exist fifty or even twenty-five years ago. In the past, the ascent to faith seemed natural, as it was woven into the fabric of family, neighborhood, village, and cultural life. One did not ask questions, for the particular religious reality was confirmed by the lifestyle, environment, context, and structure of the local community.

Rahner notes that Jesus Christ "has become the eternal restlessness of this world." It is within this restlessness where we discover that "he is with us who proclaim his resurrection: in our words, when they sound empty and tiny even to ourselves; in our blessings, even when they come forth with strain and difficulty from our lips; in our sacraments, even when they no longer seem to harbor any strength in them." Our modern-day apostolate is to speak to restlessness of the heart (Rahner, 179).

The times have changed. We find that people today are not blindly loyal to the denomination in which they were raised, and they are not hesitant about testing different churches. It is imperative, therefore, that we take a good long look at expanding our traditional understanding of positioning, imagining, or inculturating the Good News.

Please note that we are not eliminating anything we have or are doing today in our approaches for witnessing to Jesus Christ. We need, however, to expand our consciousness for thinking in terms of a "new evangelization" in style, format, and expression.

Those four "burning questions" that Pope Paul VI clearly articulated during the 1974 Synod are the stimuli and rationale for contemplating a new way for the Good News:

> In our day, what has happened to that *hidden energy of the Good News*, which is able to have a powerful effect on man's conscience?
>
> To what extent and in what way is that *evangelical force capable of really transforming the people of this century?*
>
> What *methods should be followed* in order that the power of the Gospel may have its effect?
>
> Finally, does the Church or does she not *find herself better equipped to proclaim the Gospel* and to put it into people's hearts with conviction, freedom of spirit and effectiveness? (Rahner, 179)

These questions contain a synergistic perspective for understanding our witnessing efforts, especially through the media. By reading and contemplating such phrases as "hidden energy," "powerful effect," "transforming

the people," "methods" (plural) and "conviction, freedom of spirit and effectiveness," we sense a dynamic thrust that is life-giving, enthusiastic, and renewing.

## Nurturing the Religious Imagination

While there is no single answer to the questions posed by Paul VI, there are alternative approaches that may be considered to capture the religious imagination of contemporary society. What does religious imagination mean for us?

Tracy, Hilkert, Brueggemann and others are repositioning and enriching the significance of imagination into our religious language and ministries.[6] Imagination is defined as "the act or power of forming a mental image of something not present to the senses or never before wholly perceived in reality.[7]

Imagination is an active process, which seeks ways to assist us in comprehending our experiences and the reality around us. In one sense, we can say that imagination is an individual's attempt to reach for connectedness, wholeness and meaning. The work of Daloz, Keen, Parks, and Daloz indicate the dynamic process of imagination:

> When we perceive things, we do not take them into our minds "just as they are." Rather, we compose them into internal images.

Wrapped in the senses, these perceptions, or compositions, become the stuff of feelings thought and language. The human mind is not a simple copier but rather an incessant composer, and this composing occurs through the process of imagination. . . . Since the images we take in, along with the images we compose, serve to define "how life is," they also determine "how we act". . . . "The quality of a society is dependent upon the strength of its imagination."[8]

I believe the same applies to the development of our religious imagination toward faith-filled proclamation and witnessing. Faith is a meaning-making process in our lives. So, whether we are speaking about secular or religious faith, faith is the foundation upon which we say "yes" to life. This "yes" is a profound and integrating confirmation of who we are and who we are becoming.

The idea for exploring religious imagination is pressing us to define how to reveal the "hidden energy of the Good News" and to "put it into people's hearts with conviction, freedom of spirit and effectiveness." To accomplish this task the world is in great need of "imaginers" of the Gospel, individuals who see the new methodologies (technologies) as the artistic tools to capture the religious imagination of the culture.

Schillebeeckx wrote that language becomes meaningless unless it has some reference to the existential situation. "There can, for example, be no real and meaningful possibility of people listening to the message of Christ's redemption and of their being open to give their consent to it if that message cannot be experienced and seen, in however fragmentary a way, in our existence here on earth." People today are fascinated by image, by what is visible and concrete, rather than by reason or abstract knowledge. This means we have to rediscover the image dimension of the Gospel. Since the word that moves, attracts, and empowers people is not an abstract doctrinal word but the word of story, metaphor, and image, we must recover the liberating word within all aspects of our religious experience.[9]

There is no doubt that the lives of significant individuals can nurture religious imagination and communication; actions speak louder than words. The lives of Oscar Romero, Mother Theresa, Dorothy Day, Sr. Thea

Bowman, Cardinal Joseph Bernardin, and others bestow rich and profound witness to the meaning and impact of faith alive! Life commitment to the Gospel particularly expressed through the work for social justice, racial equality, respect for life, freedom, inclusivity, and the transformation of the world continue to have a significant impact on living faith. Who or what can communicate more amid a cacophony of diverse religious and secular stories being woven into the fabric of our cultures?[10]

We realize that religious imagination is the process by which we express our experience of the presence of God. As Schillebeeckx stated, "The Gospel's message is too rich to be contained within one paradigm." There are rich symbols, words, images, and rituals that can support the articulation and animation of a religious experience and create openness to the Good News within the diverse cultural contexts of people's lives.[11]

Evangelization can be amplified, as we seek new perspectives for retelling the stories of Scripture within the human stories of today, or for disclosing the spirituality of the human situation in the light of Scripture. Jesus told the story of God by sharing ordinary human experience and transforming it through his presence of words and actions. Such storytelling may take form within and through any of the media or cybercommunities evolving today. History suggests that a new communication medium tends to complement rather than replace other media.[12]

What can be done by the Church "to be the channel of the gift of grace, to reconcile sinners with God, and to perpetuate Christ's sacrifice in the Mass, which is the memorial of his death and glorious resurrection?"[13]

# The Challenge for a New Evangelization

A kaleidoscopic approach to evangelization opens the door to a panorama of possibilities for speaking about Jesus. The goal is to utilize all the arts and senses in order to stimulate greater consciousness of our religious heritage and current reality. Critical reflection on shifting the paradigm toward kaleidoscope opportunities can offer richer insights for a new evangelization.

Poetry, drama, art, music, dance, film, videocassettes, computers, virtual reality, and the Internet are merging and converging to form new kaleidoscope patterns for capturing the imagination of youth and adults. In *The Catholic Myth*, Andrew M. Greeley contributes to the idea and methodology we seek to advance:

> Religion is an imaginative "cultural system"—a collection of directing "pictures" through which humans organize and give meaning to the phenomena that impinge on their consciousness, especially insofar as these phenomena require some explanation of the ultimate purpose of life. While these "pictures" may produce theology and ethical codes, they are prepositional and metaphorical. The codes are derivative, the superstructure built on an imaginative and preconscious infrastructure.[14]

Greeley guides us toward a renewed understanding that religion is fundamentally experience, symbol, story, and community before it becomes creed, rite, and institution (Greeley, 39). As evangelizers, we seek to nurture a foundation upon which we can weave the rich traditions of our heritage and ignite a deep faith.

As we are told in 2 Timothy to "stir into flame the gift of God," evangelizers need to look at the expanding media culture and determine how to incorporate both the new media and traditional art forms into evangelizing efforts, in order that experience, symbol, story and community can take on a richer and deeper life. While there is an urgency to ensure that content is the focus of our efforts, we must not let go of the process or the creative methods and expressions that can give new form and animation for a living faith (2 Tm 1:6).

## Kaleidoscope Considerations as We Move Forward

Time and space does not permit us to explore all the media possibilities available to us. Therefore, I confine myself to a few I feel passionate about these days because I believe they are sorely overlooked in an imaginative and pastoral way: art, radio, and the Internet.

These are not radically new media or ideas. However, I invite you to reconsider them in light of the conversations of this conference. These media may spark your religious imagination to rediscover them anew and open their doors.

## Art

Art is a rich traditional place to begin our conversation. Art has the ability to speak to all our senses and stir the inner being of our humanity.

Art as a means of evangelization and catechesis is anything but foreign to our Catholic heritage. Consider Romanesque and Gothic cathedrals, or Byzantine mosaics and icons, Michelangelo's Sistine Chapel, and so many inspiring works of art: painting, sculpture, music, poetry, and plays that speak to the human heart about God's self-communication through time and history. These works continue to touch us in ways that transcend words.

For years I have been encouraging Church leaders to reclaim the arts in a serious way as a defined or explicit ministry within the Church. What if each diocese had a Guild of Artists? A guild would enable quality religious art to be more accessible or available for diverse ministries. A guild could include a rich diversity of the arts: painters, sculptures, architects, poets, etc. We could establish an apprenticeship for new or aspiring artists in the Church. We might even go so far as to encourage each parish to have such a guild.

What would happen if we encouraged our young people to cultivate their artistic gifts for evangelization, proclaiming what they believe through art? What steps and efforts would be required of us to make this a reality? We must not limit our vision, but think creatively, boldly, and prophetically in the face of the Church's present challenges. While the Church has recognized Church musicians, there are many other art forms needing our attention.

The arts have the ability to speak to all our senses, stir the inner being, and encourage the growing spiritual quest of people. Art can be a profound means for addressing the new evangelization addressed today.

One evening while reading the *Asia Focus Newsletter,* my eyes fell upon a photograph entitled "The Incomplete Crucifix." The commentary told the story of how a priest in Korea had struggled to bring his parish together as a community. The parish's internal problems seemed insurmountable. The priest decided to commission an artist to illustrate the struggle within the community.

One Sunday when parishioners entered the church they discovered their traditional crucifix had been replaced by a new one. There was something different and strange about it. The right-side of the cross beam was missing, but Jesus' arm was stretched out in midair as if the beam were there. The left-side beam existed but the Lord's arm lay limp along the side of the body. The parishioners contemplated the meaning of this cross in silence.

The question the pastor presented to his parishioners was: "How is this crucifix representative of our parish today?" The homily the pastor gave, grounded on the art before them, deeply moved the parishioners. We are told the parish turned around and committed themselves to strengthening their parish community in the spirit of Jesus.

A sculpture by John Safer was exhibited in the Dayton Art Museum over the summer. While his work is not explicitly religious, you can feel what the artist is expressing in every piece. The sculptures capture the space around them, reaching out in soaring lines, attracting rays of light from behind like the carved lens of a telescope, and producing unusual mixtures of colors and shapes.

Safer's own interpretation of his work amplifies the observer's experience:

> Since art transcends all language barriers, as well as time and space, it is my goal—perhaps more a hope—that people now and in times to come will sense from my creations the concepts that brought them into being, and somehow feel closer to each other and to the world in which we must all try to live.[15]

Yes, art can convey the nobility of the artist's soul, raise questions about the meaning and value of life, and unite viewers in a feeling of brotherhood or love. Imagine how quality art can impact our parish space![16]

In 1999 the *National Catholic Reporter* (NCR) published *Jesus 2000*. This publication was the result of their request for artistic representations of Jesus Christ. Over 1,000 artists in nineteen countries submitted entries. The NCR special supplement included about sixty works chosen by the judges, along with a few NCR favorites. This publication continues to be a great reference for my conversations with students concerning who Jesus is for them.

The *Jesus 2000* project shows how we might use art to stimulate spiritual and religious conversations in our new evangelization efforts. Perhaps your parish could consider having a religious/spiritual art festival and inviting the local community. Workshops, seminars, or lectures on specific themes during the festival could open doors to alternative ways of speaking about Jesus.[17]

These recent personal experiences reconfirmed for me the power of art to speak to the human heart. Through art we can animate a new evangelization. Art can be a portal to "deepen the faith of Christians, forge a new culture open to the Gospel message and promote the social transformation of the continent."[18]

## Radio

Radio is a medium vastly undermined as a means of evangelization by the Church in the United States.[19]

The Paulists have made an outstanding contribution and commitment to the media in ways that are unprecedented in our American Catholic history. The Paulist radio ministry has been one of the beacons of light announcing the message of Christ. The broadcasts have spurred more than a few dioceses to consider the opportunities for radio evangelization ministry. Yet, in comparison to other parts of our Catholic world we have fallen short in our radio endeavors.

People spend enormous amounts of time listening to the radio in their cars, at work, at play, and via the Internet. Radio is a dominant means of communication in our culture, and the Church should not second-guess the power of radio to share the Gospel message.

While a few dioceses may be able to manage a large or small radio station, this is not a requirement to enter into radio ministry. Why not consider placing radio spots and programs on existing stations? If you are wondering where to begin, contact the National Catholic Academy for Communication Arts Professional. You will be connected with a wealth of Catholic professional media personnel and resources to support new initiatives in this area.

## Internet

Cyberspace is becoming the new marketplace of the twenty-first century. In the Pontifical Council for Culture's document *Toward a Pastoral Approach to Culture*, we read:

> Without doubt, the Internet's immense potential can be enormously helpful in spreading the Good News. "This has already been proved by various promising initiatives the Church has

taken, calling for a responsible creative development on this new frontier of the Church's mission."[20] A great deal is at stake. How can we not be present and use information networks, whose screens are at the heart of people's homes, to implant the values of the Gospel there?[21]

There is an exigency for evangelizers to identify new perspectives and possibilities for retelling our stories about God and humanity within this new marketplace. What can we say about this new place?

Religious presence on the web is staggering and expanding as we speak. Plug the word "God" into a Netscape search, and you'll get over 800,000 responses. A navigation through the more popular Internet search engines lists almost 18,000 sites devoted to religion and spirituality. As for the word "catholic," a search lists more than fifteen categories with over 3,700 sites. *Catholic-USA.com* lists 3,884 active Catholic links.

Every day we discover additional agencies and entrepreneurs positioning themselves in cyberspace. If this is the new marketplace of society, we need to be there evangelizing as well. With or without us, this virtual culture is being formed, and transforming all those who endeavor to navigate through its endless pathways. We have a choice: Do we see cyberspace as an alternative or additional site for evangelization and religious expressions, workshops, prayer, spiritual exercises, etc.?

If yes, how do we pursue the new evangelization we have been reflecting upon and discussing these days, in order that our place in cyberspace has impact and meaning for proclaiming the Good News?

In *Growing Up Digital: The Rise of the New Generation*, author Don Tapscott explains that in the United States in 1997, 44 percent of all households owned a computer and 60 percent of these households had children. Today it is estimated that there are over fourteen million Internet users under the age of eighteen in North America. That number is projected to grow to thirty-seven million over the next five years.[22] Keep in mind that almost every prediction concerning Internet growth has been far too low. The important point is that users are "connected" to a web of people and information that surpasses anything previously seen in human history. Users are not content to assimilate information passively, but intrigued with interacting, responding, and giving it new shape and meaning.[23]

The World Wide web has created a virtual new working and learning space for us. We find almost everything at our fingertips: libraries; bulletin boards; conference rooms (chat rooms); educational (religious and secular) opportunities; broad and diverse religious presences (via education, worship and evangelization); basic communication networks (e-mail, list serve and audio/video conferencing). One does not have to leave the comforts of school, office, or home to be navigating through billions of pages, resources, and information to support multiple research, educational, and networking needs.

In cyberspace, women, men and children converse across cultures and generations on common regional, national, and global projects of interest and concern. In a few seconds or minutes, people can be chatting online in text, uploading/downloading audio and video messages, designing plans, and sharing experiences that broaden their perception of life and faith in the global village. Navigational opportunities and resources are only limited by lack of imagination. Internet skills are becoming ordinary or normal functions for individuals who share information and position themselves in cyberspace.

While there are still many who feel that the Internet is no place for religion, evangelization, or religious experiences, and who believe that cyberspace only offers a shallow sense of religious community, I believe we need to be more open, thinking outside the box for a new time and place. I have already seen through The Virtual Learning Community for Faith Formation that communities of faith can be nurtured. I have come to firmly believe that the greater our presence in cyberspace, the greater our challenge to enhance the quality of our parish and sacramental life in our actual (real) parishes! This is not an "either/or" deal, but a "both/and." The parish needs to be ready for the personal encounter initiated in cyberspace. While people may spend a lot of time in cyberspace, a very few may be lost in cyberspace. A vast majority of individuals eventually reach out to touch in some physical way those with whom they have found a meaningful connection or encounter. Thus, it is not only important for the Church/parish to position itself in an interactive way in cyberspace but to prepare for a physically live encounter. I believe we need to continue to engage in serious thinking of what this potentially means for being and becoming Church today.[24]

The Internet—the Virtual Age—is the new missionary frontier for the Church. The World Wide web is vast and deep. Even with high-powered search engines, we cannot decipher precisely what is happening in there. The best metaphor I find to describe my own research and ministry through the web is an archeological dig. One must be persistent, patient, and profoundly investigative to explore the realms of culture forming on the Internet.

Are we willing to become pioneers of faith within the new missionary frontier? What new mindsets and skills are required? What techniques (tools) are available for us within our diocese, parish or local community? What new steps are required for us to move forward?

Although the Internet is currently the latest, hottest medium (largely because of the World Wide web), it will continue to converge with other media in the advancing years. The communication tools associated with the Internet are becoming smaller, faster, better, cheaper, and more expressive. Those who have learned to navigate through the vast regions of cyberspace find an astonishing variety of conversations taking place daily, a tropical greenhouse of discourse communities in bloom, a laboratory of extended conversations and social experiments organized around every conceivable topic and interest. The virtual age is a reality that the Church must come to terms with if our new evangelizing efforts are to have meaning and impact in the twenty-first century.[25]

A place must be cleared within this new virtual culture for the witnessing and communicating of the Gospel. If the Internet is truly forming a new culture, or a complex of cultures, it should not surprise us that people are spending more and more of their time online (interactively), and that they have begun to devise ways to fulfill the religious needs and identities that form such an important part of the fabric of our society.

In a 1990 address on *The Christian Message in a Computer Culture,* Pope John Paul II noted the revolutionary impact of contemporary developments in communication such as cyberspace: "One no longer thinks or speaks of social communications as mere instruments or technologies. Rather they are now seen as part of a still unfolding culture whose full implications are as yet imperfectly understood and whose potentialities remain for the moment only partly exploited."[26]

Since this reality is expanding at quantum speed, the Church must augment a consistent, vigilant effort. The effort is not to be considered a luxury but an essential ingredient of our evangelization efforts.

Yet the present reality indicates that the Church is woefully unprepared to effectively carry out her tasks in cyberspace. There are hundreds and thousands of Catholic websites in cyberspace. Many of these sites lack a sense of "life," invitation, or quality art, and have little or no interactivity or manifestation of freshness, renewal, or change to stimulate the religious imagination. Many websites continue to do what they currently do in print, with little or no deviation to reflect the new interactive medium. While placing information in cyberspace is a worthy beginning, life in cyberspace is dynamic, shifting, and improving every day. Our witnessing in cyberspace must be the same!

## Conclusion

If we believe that the Spirit of the Lord calls every person and each culture to its own fresh and creative response to the Good News, perhaps we need to shake off the sluggishness of time past and allow our lives to be reawakened with a new Pentecost. We are living in a *kairos* moment of history. We must bear in mind that the Gospel is too rich to be contained within only one paradigm if it is to be heard and lived with dedication, vitality, and authentic passion! We have tried to communicate in our presentation that opening our doors to diverse media and thinking outside the box offers us a kaleidoscope of opportunities to stimulate people's religious imagination and receptivity to hear and respond to Jesus Christ.

---

1   Edward Schillebeeckx, *The Language of Faith: Essays on Jesus, Theology, and the Church* (Maryknoll, NY: Orbis Press, 1995).
2   Pope John Paul II, *Communio et Progressio: On the Means of Social Communication* (Rome: May 23, 1971).
3   *Redemptoris Missio: On the Permanent Validity of the Church's Missionary Mandate* (Vatican City: December 7, 1990) and Pontifical Council for Social Communications, *Pastoral Instruction Aetatis Novae: On Social Communications on the Twentieth Anniversary of "Communio et Progressio"* (Vatican City: February 22, 1992), no. 11.
4   *General Directory for Catechesis* (Washington, DC: USCCB, 1997), 15ff.
5   Karl Rahner, *The Great Church Year: The Best of Karl Rahner's Homilies, Sermons, and Meditations*, edited by Albert Raffelt; translation edited by Harvey D. Egan. (New York: Crossroad, 1993), 7–9.
    Subsequent citations are given in text.

6   See also Walter Brueggemann, *The Prophetic Imagination*, 2nd ed. (Minneapolis: Fortress Press, 2001); Mary Catherine Hilkert, *Naming Grace: Preaching and the Sacramental Imagination* (New York: Continuum, 1997); and David Tracy, *The Analogical Imagination: Christian Theology and the Culture of Pluralism* (New York: Crossroad, 1981).

7   *The Merriam-Webster Dictionary: Home and Office Edition* (Springfield, MA: Merriam-Webster, 1998).

8   Laurent A. Park Daloz, Cheryl H. Keen, James P. Parks, and Sharon Daloz, *Common Fire: Leading Lives of Commitment in a Complex World* (Boston: Beacon Press, 1996), 132–133.

9   Schillebeeckx, *The Language of Faith*, 86.

10  There are videos documenting these great lives. Check your media libraries and references.

11  Schillebeeckx, *The Language of Faith*, 86.

12  Mary Catherine Hilkert, *Naming Grace: Preaching and the Sacramental Imagination* (New York: Continuum, 1997), 54.

13  Pope Paul VI, *Evangelii Nuntiandi: On Evangelization in the Modern World* (Washington, DC: USCCB, 1975), no. 14.

14  Andrew M. Greeley, *The Catholic Myth: The Behavior and Beliefs of American Catholics* (New York: Collier Books, 1991), 44.

15  Walter Boyne, *Art in Flight: The Sculpture of John Safer* (New York: Hudson Hills Press, 1991).

16  Earle J. Coleman, *Creativity and Spirituality: Bonds Between Art and Religion* (Albany: State University of New York Press, 1998), 13.

17  Pamela Schaeffer and John L. Allen Jr., "Jesus 2000," *National Catholic Reporter* (December 24, 1999). There are many videos produced that can advance a conversation on religion and art. Check out your diocesan media library and media resource outlets.

18  "Toward the Fifth Centenary of New World Evangelization," *Origins* 20 (September 6, 1990), 208–216.

19  Ongoing accounting of existing Catholic radio stations and programming around the world indicates the United States lags behind many other cultures in radio ministry. This has been documented by SIGNIS (Brussels).

20  Pope John Paul II, *Christifideles Laici: On the Vocation and the Mission of the Lay Faithful in the Church and in the World* (Rome: December 30, 1988).

21  Pontifical Council for Culture, *Toward a Pastoral Approach to Culture* (Vatican City, May 23, 1999), no. 9.

22  Don Tapscott, *Growing Up Digital: The Rise of the Net Generation* (New York: McGraw-Hill, 1998), 22–23.

23  Barry Muntz, "Changing Landscape," *Educause Review* (January/February 2000), 17.

24  The Virtual Learning Community for Faith Formation (VLCFF) for online adult faith experiences is designed by The Institute for Pastoral Initiatives of the University of Dayton. The VLCFF was activated in 1997. As of 2003, there are over eighteen courses and seminars available. A growing number of adults eager to learn more about the Catholic Church and strengthen their own faith are participating.

25  Stephen D O'Leary, "Cyberspace as Sacred Space," *Journal of the American Academy of Religion* (Fall, 1996).

26  Pope John Paul II, *The Christian Message in a Computer Culture* (Vatican City: January 24, 1990).

# REFLECTION QUESTIONS

If money were no object, imagine some new, uncharted ways to proclaim the Good News in our world today.

Through what medium has your own religious imagination been evoked? In your ministry, what medium have you used to evoke the religious imagination of others?

The Church exists to evangelize. In light of this priority, how is the Church better equipped to meet this challenge? What needs to change so that the Church becomes better equipped to proclaim the Gospel with conviction in the future?

---

**Angela Ann Zukowski** *is a Mission Helper of the Sacred Heart. She is the director of the Institute for Pastoral Initiatives and associate professor in the Department of Religious Studies of the University of Dayton (a Catholic/Marianist University). She is the world president for the International Catholic Association for Radio and Television known as UNDA and is a member of the Pontifical Council for Social Communications (Vatican). Currently she is working with the Federation of Asian Bishops Conference for Social Communications exploring new avenues for the use of the Internet for ministry. She is engaged in research and the design of prototypes for interactive distance learning for Catholic education and evangelization.*

# Opening Liturgy

## FINDING A WORTHY PERSON IN TODAY'S WORLD

Bishop Wilton D. Gregory • *Diocese of Belleville* • President, USCCB

F rom whence do Christians come? That is a fundamental question evidently significant enough to bring nearly five hundred people to the city of Portland for these days of interchange and encouragement. Traditionally, there have been two essential responses to that query with which most of us are familiar. The first response brings us face to face with the Church's rich missionary traditions. Christians came from the hard and faithful work of missionaries who leave home, family, culture, and often safety, to travel to distant lands where they learned new languages, met new civilizations, and eventually brought the Gospel to people living in or under pagan conditions. The second response was the one with which most of us personally are quite familiar—Catholic parents had Catholic babies and the Church continued to grow based upon the blessed fecundity of our people.

We are all here because we have come to understand that these two time-tested pathways to faith upon which we continue to rely, while they are still successful are not nearly enough in the post modern world in which we live to ensure the growth of the Church's faith. We obviously still need missionaries to leave home and hearth with the Gospel in tow. We very much still need all of our Catholic parents to bring their offspring to the Church for life with water and the Holy Spirit, but we are also living in societies that have already been evangelized and yet remain blatantly unfamiliar with the Gospel. We are also surrounded by

people who have been baptized, confirmed, and fed with the Eucharist but who do not know—and perhaps even more distressing have little desire to know—the Christ. We are called to evangelize a society that cannot adequately be called to, and transformed by, the Gospel of Jesus Christ simply by means of the two categories that we once thought covered the gamut of where Christians originated.

Like Joseph's anxious brothers, we are entering a new and perhaps dangerous arena and like them, we will possibly be surprised at what we discover. The brothers of Joseph had most likely forgotten their younger brother, or at least the pain of the memory of what they had done to their own flesh and blood caused them to repress the thought. They went into Egypt hoping to find food, perhaps a hostile environment, maybe even rejection. They had limited expectations. What they found was their past and their future tightly bound in a forgotten sibling.

The Holy Father has called the Church to a new evangelization. His summons brings us fully into the arena shared by those who are foreign missionaries. We must learn another language, discover the elements of even this secular culture that are worthy, and test the limits of a new world, even though it might appear to be a world with which we are completely familiar. To use the words of today's Gospel, we are looking for "a worthy person," a person who may not be fully aware of it, but is open to and even desirous of learning the message of Salvation. We cannot forget that there are people—a great many we all believe— in our society of secular values, who are open to the message of life and hope that is Jesus Christ. We represent many nations, some of which are Catholic by general consensus, but clearly not imbued with the spirit of the Gospel and its values.

Some of us may wonder at times how we got to where we are. We remember the days when the Church and its values enjoyed wide, if not universal, approval. More than a few bishops in the United States have paused to ask during the past year and a half: "How did we get into this situation?" The responses received have been hostile, facile, and occasionally enlightened. However we find ourselves at this moment in time and in society, it is the world into which the Lord sends us. Joseph must have wondered at times how he ended up in Egypt. It was only after he reflected in faith that he was able to accept God's providence for him and to understand that he was to become a source of hope and life for his brothers and father.

The Church's primary mission of evangelization, which is our own personal mission, cannot begin in doubt and despair. Those who are called to evangelize and, indeed, to re-evangelize our society must be people of hope. We must begin with the clear understanding that there are "worthy" people in our world who may be cynical, misguided, perhaps even hostile, but who also long to find meaning and purpose in their lives. We cannot be timid in telling and showing them that only in Christ can any of us find direction, true insight, and most importantly, real life. Ours is the complex mission of sharing that truth to a world that may think it has already heard that message before. And the greatest challenge that we face is one which all missionaries and, indeed, every parent faces: our lived witness is the only way that we can change the hearts of those we seek to convince that Christ is the only enduring and true Light of the World.

---

### READINGS
Genesis 44:18-21; 23b-29; 45:1-5 • Matthew 10:7-15

---

**Wilton D. Gregory** *is the seventh Bishop of Belleville, Illinois, and was elected president of the USCCB in November 2001. Bishop Gregory was ordained a Catholic priest for the Archdiocese of Chicago on May 9, 1973. He was appointed auxiliary bishop of Chicago on October 31, 1983, and was ordained on December 13, 1983. Prior to his episcopal ordination, he had served as an associate pastor at Our Lady of Perpetual Help Parish in Glenview, a member of the faculty at Saint Mary of the Lake Seminary in Mundelein, and a master of ceremonies to Cardinals John Cody and Joseph Bernardin.*

# General Session

## CATECHESIS: EVANGELIZING MOMENTS

### Carol Eipers, D.Min

T he Church gathered here in Portland to discuss evangelization cannot help but reflect on Jesus' words to his disciples, "Go. . . and make disciples of all nations" (Mt 28:19). If Jesus were to stand here in our midst, I wonder if he might address to us the familiar colloquial question, "What part of 'go and make disciples of all nations' don't you understand?"

Indeed, in my preparations for this institute, I have discovered that perhaps we don't understand sometimes; perhaps we even make it difficult for each other to understand our call to go—to evangelize.

I often begin a presentation by defining the terms in my title. How do you define evangelization? The Merriam-Webster dictionary says evangelize means "to preach the Gospel to; to convert to Christianity." *Evangelii Nuntiandi: On Evangelization in the Modern World* (EN) says, "For the Church, evangelizing means bringing the Good News into all the strata of humanity, and through its influence transforming humanity from within and making it new."[1]

The *Catechism of the Catholic Church* (CCC) defines evangelization as "The proclamation of Christ and his Gospel by word and testimony of life, in fulfillment of Christ's command."[2] Other documents nuance the definition and finally *Evangelii Nuntiandi* (EN) cautions us, "Any partial and fragmentary definition which attempts to render the reality of evangelization in all its richness, complexity and dynamism does so only at the risk of impoverishing it and even of distorting it" (no.17).

I was chatting with a fellow airline passenger who inquired about the topic of my presentation here in Portland. When I answered "Evangelization!" he asked what my quota was. "All nations," I replied and he looked impressed! Jesus set the quota.

Catechesis has as many definitions as there are documents that address this essential ministry. The *Catechism of the Catholic Church* defines catechesis as, "An education of children, young people, and adults in the faith of the Church through the teaching of Christian doctrine in an organic and systematic way to make them disciples of Jesus Christ"(no. 189). The *General Directory for Catechesis* (GDC) seems to broaden this definition in saying, "Catechesis is nothing other than the process of transmitting the Gospel, as the Christian community has received it, understands it, celebrates it, lives it and communicates it in many ways."[3]

*Catechesi Tradendae* names catechesis "a very remarkable moment in the process of evangelization."[4] "Moment" according to the Merriam-Webster dictionary is a noun: a minute portion of time, present time, a time of excellence or conspicuousness. Is catechesis only one moment? Is evangelization a one-time process that one "graduates" from? Are all evangelists catechists? Are all ministries catechesis? Recently I saw a book entitled, *It's Hard to Make a Difference When You Can't Find Your Keys.* That is how I feel sometimes. It is hard to transform the world if I am still defining my work.[5]

Again I hear Jesus, "Go and make disciples." I have to have some answers though, Jesus, in order to do what you ask. I understand, from Scripture and Tradition that the Church exists in order to evangelize (EN no. 14). Each of the ministries of the Church, therefore, exists in order to evangelize. Evangelization is not merely "another lens" through which we view our various ministries. It is the mission and measure of all that we do. Catechesis is part of evangelization; therefore, each ministry also serves to catechize. We all share the one mission of the Church, and the structures we design and ministerial boundaries we set sometimes preclude the generous sowing of the word which the Gospel demands. We can give the impression that evangelization is an elitist role rather than a baptismal responsibility. "I will make you fishers of people" Jesus promised (Mt 4:19). We are to cast the net—imagine the paltry catch if each of us insisted on using just "my" piece of the net.

The relationship of evangelization and catechesis can be understood in terms of human relationships. Indeed the goal of both evangelization and catechesis is relationship: with God the Father, Son, and Holy Spirit, and with the Church. Evangelization is the initial encounter—I am attracted, perhaps it is even "love at first sight." Catechesis deepens this initial attraction through knowledge and experiences of the beloved until it matures into commitment of life. As in all human relationships, this loving more, learning more, being attracted more deeply is not linear, but spiraling and lifelong.

Evangelization and catechesis are inseparable in three ways: first, those who evangelize must be catechized in order to proclaim the Gospel faithfully and fully; second, those who are evangelized need catechesis to deepen their love and understanding of God and the Church. Finally, there is what *Evangelii Nuntiandi* calls "the test of truth, the touchstone of evangelization" (no. 24). The evangelized and catechized go on to evangelize others.

And Jesus says—do you hear him?—"Go and make disciples." Enough of the defining and intellectualizing: "Go and make disciples!" For two thousand years we have been at it; for the last decades we have generated a library of documents defining and strategizing and outlining plans. Just evangelize!

A new church in New York does it. I have received postcards every few weeks that capture my attention—and invite me. Many people were evangelizing in New York City in the weeks following September 11, 2001. They were on street corners, distributing pamphlets of prayers and inviting people to their churches; they were leading prayer on street corners and at the memorials that sprung up all over town. Personally, I did not witness any Catholics in these efforts, but they may have been there. I was personally invited to join six other churches though.

Maybe the first word we should be defining and teaching and living as a Church is "Go!" Maybe we should be doing some things differently. If we are to "Go and make disciples" we are called to the new evangelization. But the new evangelization calls for new catechesis as well, one that is clearly focused on the mission of the Church: to evangelize. The six fundamental tasks of catechesis detailed in the *General Directory for Catechesis* give us a framework to talk about what we can do (nos. 85-86).

## Knowledge of the Faith

The first task of catechesis is promoting knowledge of the faith. *Catechesi Tradendae* (CT) reminds us that the faith is not a what but a who. "At the heart of catechesis we find, in essence, a Person, the Person of Jesus of Nazareth"(no. 5). Seeing this task in the light of evangelization means that we are consciously forming evangelizers. Those we teach need the words to articulate the faith, they need to develop skills in celebrating and sharing the Good News, and they need opportunities to practice witnessing to Jesus in their lives and decisions. Knowledge is not the end. As the Prologue to the *Catechism* reminds us, "The whole concern of doctrine and its teaching must be directed to the love that never ends" (no. 25). Knowledge is a foundation for love and love impels us to share the one whom we have come to know and love. Knowledge enables us to share Jesus with those who do not know him; knowledge enables us to explain the truths of faith and the teachings of the Church to those who search for God. Go! As Peter implores us "Always be ready to give an explanation to anyone who asks you for a reason for your hope…" (1 Pt 3:15).

## Liturgical Education

The second task is liturgical education. The liturgy is the Church's work of art. In liturgy we meet Jesus and we express our faith in color and the ageless symbols of water, fire, oil, bread, and wine. We pray with images and ritual gesture, in words and music and dance. In liturgy we move to the symphony of faith in ways deeper than daily life allows.

Seeing liturgical education as evangelization means we are aware of who celebrates with us and who does not. Be on the lookout for those who are present but not yet initiated into the Catholic Church. Catechesis not only must prepare the catechized to participate in liturgy but enable them to help others participate. Catechesis announces a Kingdom of God that is inclusive and urges us to welcome everyone. Yet I have

> "We are entering a period of new vitality for the
> Church, a period in which adult Catholic laity
> will play a pivotal leadership role in
> fulfilling the Christian mission of evangelizing
> and transforming society."

*Our Hearts Were Burning Within Us:*
*A Pastoral Plan for Adult Faith Formation In the United States*
(Washington, DC: USCCB Publishing, 2000), 10.

known widows who are one-person families and single people who feel excluded by "Family Mass" at their parish.

Evangelizers know the cultures of those they serve and listen to those who can inculturate the liturgical experience. I have known parishes where the population is 60 percent Latino and no liturgy is celebrated in Spanish. Go, reach to touch and invite those who are alienated or isolated by illness or sorrow. Find those who seek God and bring them home.

Catechesis in preparation for the Sacraments is a time rich in evangelizing moments. Sometimes I ask at parish sacramental preparation sessions, "How many of these parents and guardians are unchurched or not Catholic?" The answer is usually something like, "Oh, it doesn't matter, they all have to come." Oh, but it does matter a great deal if we know that we are evangelizers. And if we are evangelizers, we bring the broader sense of sacramentality with us to share with others. We see the hand of God in all people and places and events. We can help others to see him.

On an archaeological dig in Mallorca, Spain, I was reminded of the experience of the liturgy. Every time we would unearth a fragment of pottery or a bead, the archaeologist would call everyone together and tell the story of what we had found: its age and use and what the people were like who fashioned it. The story gave meaning to the find. The Word we hear in liturgy, the prayers we pray together give meaning to

59

all that we have "dug up" through a week of life. We can see all of the fragments of our lives in the light of the Paschal Mystery.

As Pope John Paul II wrote in his encyclical letter *Ecclesia de Eucharistia: On the Eucharist*, "In the humble signs of bread and wine, changed into his body and blood, Christ walks beside us as our strength and our food for the journey, and he enables us to become, for everyone, witnesses of hope."[6]

## Moral Formation

The third task of catechesis is moral formation. Catholic morality is first of all a positive belief about who we are and our purpose in this life. Our worth does not change with the market. We are created in the image and likeness of God, redeemed by God's only Son, our brother Jesus. We are temples of the Holy Spirit, embraced by a community of faith and supported by a communion of saints.

But Catholic morality teaches us to honor the equal dignity of all people. We therefore put out the welcome mat for everyone, inviting everyone and offering to help with whatever burdens they may bear. If we are witnessing to Catholic morality our parishes will be safe places. Safe, and accessible to those who are poor, to those who are challenged by disabilities, to those who are rejected. If we are not welcoming and safe and accessible for these people, how can we invite them? And if we do not invite, what is evangelization?

Catechesis is to equip us with knowledge of the commandments and the Beatitudes. It is to provide ways and opportunities to practice the virtues. Catechesis attends to forming that imagination so that we can see how to live Jesus' teachings in a contemporary society. Moral formation is also about sin—not only personal sin but also social sin and our responsibility to stand against systemic evils.

As a junior high teacher in our parish school, I remember vividly my students' shock when their "Respect All Life" messages were not applauded at our local train station. I recall how they grappled with what it means to live the Gospel values beyond their parochial classroom. The conversion that is the intent of evangelization and catechesis is a turning to God not only of our hearts, but of our lives and our public behavior.

Go! Witness outside the safe confines of the parish, which is where your life can evangelize others. And witness to the mercy of God and the mission of the Church as reconciler.

We have to teach that witness in public arenas is indispensable for the mission of the Church. One website I visited lists "Twelve Painless Ways to Evangelize." "Painless" is a curious adjective for the work of those who follow one who was crucified for the Good News he brought. The web article says, "Many of these techniques can be performed from the comfort and privacy of your own home." I think moral formation in the catechesis of evangelizers ought not to pretend that evangelizing is either comfortable or private. This is not to say that those who are at home cannot evangelize. However, of the "Twelve Painless Ways," only one involved any personal contact. Of course, the Holy Spirit can—and does—act though anonymous gestures. But Jesus says, "Go!"[7]

# Prayer

The fourth task of catechesis is teaching to pray. Catechesis teaches the two skills for prayer: speaking and listening. It should teach the prayers of the community and of the Liturgy so that we feel and can share a sense of belonging. Teaching to pray means exposing the catechized to the many ways of prayer: vocal prayer and silent meditation, contemplation, and spontaneous prayer. We can share the many cultural expressions of prayer and the devotions that are indigenous to various peoples.

Prayer is the daily bread of faith and it keeps the light of God's love alive in us. Prayer keeps us grateful. It nourishes our relationship with God and attunes us to God's call this day.

Often I hear God's voice again pleading, "Go!" We pray for those whom we might evangelize; we pray for the wisdom to share the Good News in ways that will speak to people's hearts. We pray for the courage to invite others to prayer.

## Education for Community Life

Catechesis has a fifth fundamental task: to provide education for community life. This task is two-fold. We welcome the gifts of each member, affirm and celebrate their uniqueness. This is the community gathered to support and encourage each one's faith. At the same time, we call all the baptized to stretch their sense of who "we" are, embracing all God's children as brothers and sisters. This "stretching" in the community is meant to be, and to proclaim, a place of belonging for all who desire to serve the Lord. The reality of community within the Catholic Church is especially countercultural in an age of extreme individualism.

Sometimes we are discouraged that the community is not as it ought to be. We have our expectations and the ideals of Jesus to live up to. But education for community life prepares us to live as a sinner among sinners, always seeking the Lord's forgiveness. We cannot invite others to a community which we judge and find wanting.

Go! Invite those who are alone or rejected or lost to a community where no one gets voted out. A community where gifts are acknowledged as graces of the Holy Spirit given, not for personal stardom, but as Paul says, "for the common good" (1 Cor 12:7). "Go, make disciples," use the Internet to connect with those who are distant physically or spiritually. Use your website to initiate conversation with the community of faith and to share the Good News of Jesus-in-our-midst.

# Missionary Initiation

The sixth task for catechesis is missionary initiation. One might consider that this sixth task is the purpose of the other five. All of catechesis is to continually prepare us for the mission of evangelization. The *General Directory for Catechesis* in addressing missionary initiation says:

> The evangelical attitudes which Jesus taught his disciples when he sent them on mission are precisely those which catechesis must nourish: to seek out the lost sheep, proclaim and heal at the same time, to be poor, without money or knapsack; to know how to accept rejection and persecution; to place one's trust in the Father and in the support of the Holy Spirit; to expect no other reward than the joy of working for the Kingdom (no. 86).

The development of these attitudes is the measure of effective catechesis. As Pope John Paul II said this year in one of his Mission Sunday messages, "Every member of the faithful is called to holiness and to mission."[8]

Growth in personal holiness is essential for our mission and is a result of our mission as well. The Catholic, born again of water and the Spirit in Baptism, attests to his or her belief by continuing to bring others to that new life in Christ. Evangelized and catechized, we are to embody our belief and express it in word and witness to evangelize others.

The Church has one mission: evangelization. Evangelization is accomplished by the Holy Spirit through a variety of means and ministries, one of which is catechesis. Catechesis has six tasks, which form people as disciple-evangelizers. But Jesus' demand for us to "Go!" grows more insistent in an age of violence and terrorism, in a time of war and fear. The one mission of the Church faces particular challenges that we must meet if we are to respond to Jesus.

*Evangelii Nuntiandi* says,

> The power of evangelization will find itself considerably diminished if those who proclaim the Gospel are divided among themselves in all sorts of ways. . . . Indeed, if the Gospel we proclaim is seen to be rent by doctrinal disputes, ideological polarizations or mutual condemnations among Christians. . . . Yes, the destiny of evangelization is certainly bound up with the witness of unity given by the Church (no. 77).

While these words speak to us of the divisions among Christians that are also our concern, they are addressed to the divisions within the Church as well. Turfs and competition among ministers or ministries weakens us and the mission we serve. If our structures or the people in them do not witness to the unity of the Body of Christ, they must be changed.

"Evangelizing is in fact the grace and vocation proper to the Church, her deepest identity" (EN, no. 14). Evangelization, and the catechesis that deepens it, must be the clear priority of the diocese, the parish, the institutions and services of that Church. We measure the priority we assign to things by looking at our financial expenditures, the allocation of personnel, the ways we spend our time. If evangelization is to hold the first place, we must reassess all of these items at every level of the Church. Holding tenaciously to a priority requires accountability for that priority. If we are to hold ourselves and others accountable for the mission of evangelization we have to choose appropriate measures. We cannot allow evangelization to be one-among-many ministries; it must be the very air that we live and breathe if we are to be faithful to the Church's mission.

We have to constantly echo Jesus' words to one another, "Go and make disciples." Perhaps the liturgy should end with "Go to love and serve and proclaim the Lord." Dare we end with, "Go and make disciples!"? This implies that we will define the "good parish" and the "good parishioner" differently.

A good parish gathers the community for worship and catechesis where the members are nourished for the mission. A good parish then sends the community to nourish others with the Word and through their witness. And, of course, to bring others back to the community to worship and learn.

In *Ecclesia in America: The Church in America* Pope John Paul II wrote,

> In catechesis it will be useful to keep in mind, especially on a continent like America where the social question takes on such importance, that "growth in the understanding of the faith and its practical expression in social life are intimately connected. Efforts made to favor an encounter with Christ cannot fail to have a positive repercussion in the promotion of the common good in a just society" (no. 69).

Perhaps the "good parish" can only be determined by whether the neighborhood is a better place because the parish is there.

The document *Go and Make Disciples* says that evangelization means "bringing the Good News of Jesus into every human situation and seeking to convert individuals and society by the divine power of the Gospel itself" (no. 10). If we are to affect individuals and society, we need to move beyond "parallelism." If there is a local women's or men's club, we have a Catholic one; if there are organizations formed, we have a separate one for Catholics. I realize the importance of Catholic identity in an age of pluralism. I value the contributions of so many Catholic groups. I wonder, however, when Catholics can bring the Gospel to wider areas of public life. Certainly, we Catholics all hunger for ongoing evangelization and the new evangelization calls us to attend to those in our midst whose faith has grown cold, but that is not all we are called to do. When do we go beyond the confines of our own community and its internal issues when our calendars are filled with parish or diocesan organizations and events?

You are the light of the world. What are the bushel baskets that keep that light hidden from the world? Maybe we are the ones who have woven those concealing baskets for ourselves and for others. Have we overemphasized the gathering of the community to the neglect of its

sending? And this being sent presumes that I am catechized and able to articulate, make decisions based on, and act on what we believe as Catholics.

*Evangelii Nuntiandi* says "every effort must be made to ensure a full evangelization of culture, or more correctly, of cultures. They have to be regenerated by an encounter with the Gospel. But this encounter will not take place if the Gospel is not proclaimed" (no. 20). We have to attend to cultures if we are to proclaim the Gospel in ways meaningful to people's lives. The image of media personnel being "embedded with troops" in Iraq is one that might be considered an evangelistic posture. We do not, however, put the Gospel and cultures together so that the Gospel can be revised to accommodate our lifestyles.

How do we maintain a presence in the marketplace that is faithful? Again, unless we have been catechized, we lose our voice. We are to evangelize culture, not be co-opted by it.

I was asked to address "Catechesis: Evangelizing Moments." The more I re-read and reflected on the Scriptures and the documents on evangelization and catechesis, the clearer "Go and make disciples!" rang in my ears and in my heart. And the more I realized that unless we are continually called to the mission of evangelization, there is no need for catechesis. Unless we are catechized, evangelization is weakened. The more evangelization becomes the clear priority of the Church, the more essential effective catechesis becomes and the more we will desire to be catechized.

The final point I would make then is a call to reorder our priorities—our real, operative priorities—in response to the Lord's mandate "Go and make disciples."

What's wrong with evangelization? I am. Perhaps you are. We are wrong inasmuch as we have not accepted evangelization as our personal mission. We are wrong insofar as we have not been catechized and catechized others to do that mission. We are wrong insofar as we have allowed personal agendas and opinions to take precedence over what is best for the mission of Jesus Christ.

The *Catechism* reminds us that "each believer is a link in the great chain of believers" (no. 166). But that white baptismal garment is the promise of eternal life for all the saints, if we live that new life in Christ and share it.

"Go and make disciples of all nations," the words of Jesus echo ever more insistently. "Go!" The work of Jesus is in our hands.

1   Pope Paul VI, *Evangelii Nuntiandi: On Evangelization in the Modern World* (Washington, DC: USCCB, 1975), Sec. 18.
    Subsequent citations are given in text.
2   *Catechism of the Catholic Church*, 2nd ed. (Washington, DC: USCCB: 1997), 887.
    Subsequent citations are given in text.
3   *General Directory for Catechesis* (Washington, DC: USCCB, 1988), 100–105.
4   Pope John Paul II, *Catechesi Tradendae: On Catechesis in Our Time* (Washington, DC: USCCB, 1979), no. 108.
5   Marilyn Bayfield, Ph.D., *It's Hard to Make a Difference When You Can't Find Your Keys: The Seven Step Path to Becoming Truly Organized* (New York: Viking, 2003).
6   Pope John Paul II, *Ecclesia de Eucharistia: On the Eucharist.* (Washington, DC: USCCB, 2003), Sec. 62–68.
7   See *http://www.catholic.com/library/12_ways.asp*. Catholic Answers, 2000.
8   Pope John Paul II, *Redemptoris Missio: On the Permanent Validity of The Church's Missionary Mandate.* (Washington, DC: USCCB, 1990).

# REFLECTION QUESTIONS

Carol Eipers states that although evangelization is the primary mission of the Church, it is not reflected sufficiently in our liturgies, catechesis, and stewardship. What are the most functional steps that the Church— on a national, diocesan, or parish level—takes to make the theological priority a mission priority?

How can we take the six tasks of catechesis as outlined in the *General Directory for Catechesis* to heart? How are these tasks part of our daily lived experience? Which of the six tasks finds a home in you? Which one challenges you?

How comfortable are we with the Jesus we are called to know and share? If evangelization is neither comfortable or private, what will make it so appealing that we will dedicate our lives to this mission? Are our homes, work places, parishes better places because we are there?

---

**Carole Eipers** *is the director of catechetics for William H. Sadlier, Inc. She served in parish ministries for over twenty years as a teacher, director of religious education, youth minister, and pastoral associate. She was director of the Office for Catechesis in Chicago for nine years and also served as president of the National Conference of Catechetical Leadership. She has been a member of the faculties of Mundelein Seminary, Loyola Chicago, and Loyola New Orleans, and she has written and presented extensively in the area of catechetics.*

# General Session

## CATHOLIC YOUTH EVANGELIZATION: A METHOD TO THE MADNESS

### Robert J. McCarty, D.Min

As Scripture says:

> For "everyone who calls on the name of the Lord will be saved." But how can they call on him in whom they have not believed? And how can they believe in him of whom they have not heard? And how can they hear without someone to preach? And how can people preach unless they are sent? As it is written, "How beautiful are the feet of those who bring [the] good news!" (Rom 10:13–15)

I am very grateful to have this wonderful opportunity to share some good news! This morning I would like to address three objectives:

- Identify characteristics of the spirituality of young people
- Describe three critical factors affecting the evangelization of young people
- Propose an effective process for the evangelization of young people

First, I would like to set the context. There is a spiritual reawakening going on in America. George Gallup believes that the United States is experiencing a spiritual re-awakening unparalleled in our history, spearheaded by youth and young adults. Gallup states that one in three young people by age sixteen report a significant, personal experience of God.

However, I wonder if young people have a language to talk about that experience. Do they have a community of faith that can help them understand that experience, provide a context and a tradition? This has significant implications for how we evangelize young people.[1]

## Characteristics of the Spirituality of Young People

Young people today are not angry with, or mistrustful of, organizations and institutions. They are, however, increasingly apathetic and disconnected from organizations. Spiritually, they are:

- Believers in God, though not necessarily members of particular institutions and denominations
- Involved in an individual spiritual journey, not the communal tradition
- Spiritual, but not necessarily religious

The emphasis seems to be on a vertical spirituality, a "me and God" spirituality. However, young people are open to and hungry for an experience of the holy. In an age that emphasizes "virtual reality," young people do:

- Desire a faith that makes a difference in their lives, provides meaning, purpose, and challenge
- Desire a genuine experience of the transcendence and power of God
- Relate to a Jesus who understands suffering
- Want to grow in faith together with their peers and with trusted adults
- Believe that everything expresses the transcendent: nature, the arts, gatherings, traditional devotionals[2]

So, it is apparent that the question is no longer, "Will our children have faith?" They are spiritually hungry and looking for a faith that makes sense, a faith that provides meaning and purpose, that works for them. Rather, the question is, "Will our faith have children?"

Our youth (and our adults as well) live in a voluntary world and worship in a voluntary church. Therefore, they will go where their needs are met and their hungers are fed. People are practicing theology with their feet by going where their needs are met.

Young people join cults, movements, and para-churches not primarily because of their belief systems, but because of what these organizations claim to provide:

- Experienced identity and meaning
- Instant friendships and belonging
- A sense of community
- A source of energy and enthusiasm
- A sense of belonging to a group with a mission

What does this say about young people's experience of the parish faith community? What does this say about the image and message of the Church? How are we proclaiming, connecting, and challenging young people? The fact that many young people leave the Catholic Church for other movements highlights our failure to communicate the fullness of the Gospel message of integral faith and justice.

The agenda and issues we must confront in the next few years will flow from three primary issues:

- How do we proclaim the Good News in a language young people understand?
    *Answer*: "Come and see."
- How do we connect young people to the faith community and to its mission?
    *Answer*: "Belong and share in the life of the community."
- How do we call young people to the challenge of discipleship?
    *Answer*: "Go and be disciples."

# Factors Affecting the Evangelization of Young People

In order to be a Church where the Good News is experienced as a gift, we must take stock of ourselves and undergo an examination of conscience in three arenas.

*Arena One: The Universal Church*

The first arena is the universal Church. The Church as an institution has a major image problem, in addition to the sexual abuse scandals. What the Church is *against* is often more clear than what it is *for*. People know that the Church is against married clergy, women priests, birth control, abortion, and pre-marital sex. Young people know what the Church is against. But do they know what it is the Church stands for? Do they know that the Church represents justice, compassion, healing, life, the sacramental world, the incarnation of the Kingdom of God?

The Church has an active role in bringing warring factions to the peace table; in the work of Catholic Relief Services or the Catholic Campaign for Human Development; in the service of our hospitals, schools, youth ministry, and religious education programs. But that's not what gets the press today.

What message do we give about the Church as an institution? How do we proclaim what the Church is for? For we are the Church.

This image problem is compounded by a cancer in our Church that will make evangelization more difficult: the increase in pedophilia and sexual abuse is a virus that is driving families out of the Church, especially if not dealt with in an honest, direct, and compassionate manner. And this cancer causes us to be more careful and less comfortable with our young people!

In my parish in Baltimore, I have seen the pain of youth who are scared and confused. One young person said recently that she is "embarrassed to be Catholic."

*Arena Two: The Parish Community*

The second arena in which the Church needs to re-evaluate itself is the parish community. The faith community is the context in which the Good News is best understood and proclaimed. The community prepares the soil for the "seed," nurtures the seed, and allows for conversion, which is the outcome of evangelization. The community not only proclaims the Good News intentionally, but is challenged to be the Good News in living out the Gospel message.

So the faith community is challenged to both tell the story and to be the story, to be a witness. What message does our faith community project now? "Come and be happy?" Or, "Come and be quiet, bored, sad, a spectator rather than a participant?" Where's the joy of Jesus?

72

Now, lest we get too serious, listen to these messages taken from actual parish bulletins

- The ladies of the church have cast off clothing of every kind, and they can be seen in the church basement Friday afternoon.
- Remember in prayer the many who are sick of our Church and community.
- For those of you who have children and don't know it, we have a nursery downstairs.
- The choir will meet at the Larsen house for fun and sinning.
- Don't let worry kill you off! Let the Church help.
- Next week's presentation is "What is hell?" Come early and hear the choir practice.
- There is a meeting of young mothers on Sunday night. If you'd like to be a young mother, please see Fr. John after Mass.
- And my own pastor on the Feast of Mary: "Please welcome our celebrant, Fr. Bob, with 'Hail, Holy Queen.'"

The life of the evangelizing community is critical. In our schools, parishes, and community centers we must learn to

- Create a sense of discipleship, of doing faith. What is the quality of our social outreach?
- Invite and welcome young people. In our parish we have set a goal of greeting each youth by name as they arrive for liturgy.
- Find opportunities to build relationships, which are at the core of effective ministry.
- Assess how we provide hospitality.
- Evaluate the quality of our worship. Is our liturgy alive and vibrant? In our parish we incorporate commissionings for retreats, conferences, and workcamps, an annual blessing of car keys, the annual World Youth Day celebration, and a special Graduation Mass into our weekly worship.
- Foster participation and belonging. Are youth invited into pastoral and liturgical ministries and parish councils?

This has to happen in our larger faith community and in our base communities: the religious ed classes, youth groups, confirmation programs, high schools, everywhere young people gather! Evangelization is most effective when young people feel welcomed into a living faith community and are able to interact on a personal and social level, where they experience the satisfaction of their basic needs of security, trust, acceptance, and support. The love of God is best proclaimed and most strongly grasped when young people experience human love and acceptance in the context of a vibrant faith community.

*Arena Three: Ourselves as Ministers of the Church*

Our third arena of introspection must be ourselves. The Lord's proclamation of the Good News begins with us, the ministers in the Church, both youth and adults!

Do we act redeemed? Are we in relationship with Jesus? Is this expressed in our willingness to share our gifts and talents with young people, and in our commitment to young people and their sacredness?

Young people know when we are really committed to them! But young people watch us—all of us, not just the youth ministers. Our young people watch us. Have you ever had your young people role play you? They highlight all our foibles and weird mannerisms, but I believe they also notice all our positive characteristics as well: the expressions of concern, the random acts of kindness, the comments of care and love. Our efforts do not go unnoticed!

Do we believe in something that helps us make sense of our lives? Does our faith work for us? Is faith expressed in living just lifestyles? We are visible signs of the Church, we are the reign of God present, even as the reign is continually being built up. We may be the only Gospel that some young people ever read.

We are all challenged to be visible signs of God's love for our youth! This responsibility falls not just to youth ministers, religious educators, or family life ministers, but to all of us. As in the African proverb, "It takes a village to raise a child," it takes an entire parish to nurture faith. We must be a community of people that celebrates the Good News, that proclaims the Good News of Jesus, and that lives the story and message of Jesus.

> "*Young people of every continent, do not be afraid to be the saints of the new millennium! Be contemplative, love prayer; be coherent with your faith and generous in the service of your brothers and sisters, be active members of the Church and builders of peace.*"

Pope John Paul II
15th World Youth Day, Rome
Palm Sunday, 2000

Pope Paul VI said in *Evangelii Nuntiandi: On Evangelization in the Modern World* (EN), "Modern man listens more willingly to witnesses than to teachers, and if he does listen to teachers, it is because they are witnesses." Young people today need to hear the story of Jesus, the story of the reign of God (no. 41).

But telling the story of Jesus is not a simple task. It requires preparation. Because what do you get when you cross a Seventh Day Adventist with a Roman Catholic? You get someone who loves to knock on doors, but doesn't know what to say when someone answers!

If we knock on the doors and hearts of young people, they will answer. Will we then know what to say? We have to be in touch with our stories, who we are as story. We need to be able to say "How am I different because of Jesus?" We must be able to answer the following questions:

- Why do I go to Mass?
- Why am I Catholic?
- What do I know about Jesus?

We have to be able to tell the Jesus story (not tell *about* the Jesus story). It's our challenge to be evangelists, to tell the story.

Our story is unbelievable! Who would believe Moses, Jesus, even Mother Teresa or Oscar Romero or Dorothy Day or Fr. Michael Judge (at the World Trade Center on 9/11) today? Who would believe our stories?

We have to integrate the Jesus story and his message in all aspects of our ministry:

- We can't have retreats that don't present the Jesus story
- We can't have service projects that don't mention the Gospel as their rationale
- We shouldn't run overnight ski trips, camping trips and the like and not include liturgy or prayer experiences

Evangelization is the energizing core of all our ministry, in all our settings.

## A Process for Evangelization

Before describing a simple framework for reaching out to and evangelizing young people, I need to make a distinction between "unchurched" and "ungospeled" young people. I think of "unchurched" as those young people completely unconnected or only minimally connected to a faith community. "Ungospeled" are those young people already present in our faith communities, who may never have truly experienced the Good News of the Gospel. They have never experienced the joy, the love, the peace, and the challenge of the Gospels.

Our outreach and ministry is to both groups and our approach is based on the ministry of Jesus. He ministered by first spending time where people gathered—where they worked, lived, played, worshipped, and celebrated. He then invited people into a relationship, connecting people with himself and with other believers. From these connections came the possibility of commitment. Therefore, effective outreach begins by making contact with young people.

## Contact

There are four basic ways to make contact with young people:

1. *Be where they are.* The Church, through her ministers, has to be where young people are. It's the theology of geography—we need to be the

Good News in the flesh and in the right settings. That means we need to be present where young people gather in their communities and schools, attend their events and activities. And why? Because to do so says that their space is holy ground.

2. *Establish a reputation as parishioner-friendly or youth-friendly.* The Church as parish, school, and diocese needs to build a reputation as youth-friendly. Our parish bulletins, diocesan newspapers, bulletin boards, gathering space, our budgets, and our parish life give clear messages about whether young people are valued here.

3. *Encourage others to make contact* (outreach). We need to challenge young people to reach out to their friends and to invite them into the community.

4. *Go to young people who can't come to us.* We need to extend our ministry of presence to those young people in the hospital, in detention centers, shelters, treatment programs, and in migrant camps.

## Connect

Effective contact with young people results in relationships and connections, which are at the heart of ministry with young people. There are three arenas in which we can build connections with young people:

- In personal relationships. We are challenged to connect young people with their peers and with caring, believing adults.

- With the faith community. We are challenged to foster responsible participation in the life, work, and mission of the community.
- With Jesus. At the heart of evangelization is connecting young people with the person of Jesus.

Forming connections in these three arenas is not a linear process. Each of the three may be a starting point for a young person to be connected in the other two arenas.

## Commitment

When we make contact with young people and form connections in the three arenas, we create the possibility of commitment. Commitment is certainly a free choice, a personal decision. But that decision is greatly enhanced and supported when young people are connected to the faith community and in relationship with Jesus. And only then can that relationship with Jesus be lived out in faithful discipleship.

I believe that young people are looking for a noble adventure. They want and need to hear our stories. The church has to tap into the energy, enthusiasm, and idealism of young people.

In Stowe, Vermont, I was watching teenagers ski and snowboard down a very challenging mountain and listening to them in the gondola as we headed back up for another run. I was struck by their energy, their excitement, and their sense of "reckless abandonment." They seemed to literally throw themselves down the mountain. No mountain was too high or too steep for them.

I was very aware that this reckless abandonment, this unbridled joy in the challenge, was a gift to me and to the community. I wanted to warn the young people to be careful, go slow, look both ways, check health and collision insurance. They reminded me of my own youthful optimism and dreams. I prayed that they would never lose that reckless abandonment (within limits), that no mountain would ever be too high and no slope too steep for them, and that when confronted with the challenge of the mountain of poverty, hunger, racism, or injustice, the same sense of reckless abandonment would carry them through.

The challenge in youth ministry is to harness that energy, that reckless abandonment, and infuse it with grace and faith and the Gospel.

## Challenges

I conclude this presentation with five challenges:

1. Proclaim the Good News, and proclaim it again. Young people need to hear Jesus' message of the reign of God and they need to hear our faith stories and traditions. Young people can be challenged to see the world through the lens of faith and begin to differentiate between the societal dream and the Jesus dream. Indeed, they are hungry for a dream that captures their imagination. They need to enter into a relationship with Jesus. The Church needs to be countercultural, especially recapturing its social justice values, a noble adventure!

2. Connect young people to the life of the faith community. Young people have a need to belong to something bigger than themselves and a right to responsible participation in the faith community. They must be connected to faith-filled adult role models and use their gifts on behalf of the community. They need a place where they can ask their questions, express their doubts, and live out their convictions.

3. Challenge young people to become disciples, followers of Jesus, and active participants in building the reign of God. We must call young people to this worthwhile adventure. Youth want to be committed, they want to be aligned with a community of committed believers, and they want to live out this commitment as disciples.

4. Give young people the opportunity to serve. Young people have done extraordinary things for their community through service. Their idealism and boundless energy enables them to tackle very difficult issues. They increase self esteem, confidence, and enduring belief through service and compassion. The young will begin to develop the values of the reign of God.

5. Create a parish where the Jesus dream is realized.

Have young people been sold the wrong dream? Have they been sold the societal dream of materialism, individualism, consumerism, and hedonism?

That's not the Jesus dream nor the dream of the reign of God as found in the Gospel of Luke, Chapter 4, in which Jesus quotes Isaiah in the synagogue, surrounded by the teachers, the rabbis, and the faithful:

> "The Spirit of the Lord is upon me, because he has anointed me to bring glad tidings to the poor. He has sent me to proclaim liberty to captives and recovery of sight to the blind, to let the oppressed go free, and to proclaim a year acceptable to the Lord."
> . . . He said to them, "Today this scripture passage is fulfilled in your hearing." (Lk 4:18-19, 21)

The reign of God has arrived in Christ Jesus himself. The poor, the captives, the blind, the oppressed, are found today in the developing world, in the Sudan, Iraq, Afghanistan, and in our own cities and in the rural areas of our country. They are found in some of our young people, and they are found in our own lives. We have all at one time or another been emotionally poor, if not economically so. We have all been captive to unhealthy pursuits, relationships, or values. We have all been blind to the problems of injustice around us, and to the presence of God around us. We have all been oppressed by unjust systems, others' expectations, and painful experiences in our lives.

To all of us, Jesus proclaims a year acceptable to the Lord, a Year of Jubilee, a Year of Amnesty. The reign of God is breaking through, Jesus says, and the reign of God is characterized by fullness of life with God, and a fullness of life for all God's people who are loved unconditionally by the One who created them.

This is the Jesus we are proclaiming, the story we are telling. This is the Jesus who moves us!

It's the Jesus who stands up in the synagogue with the courage and the conviction to announce the reign of God. It's the Jesus who responds to young people's hungers: for meaning, recognition, belonging, justice, and holiness. It's the Jesus who heals our humanity, who responds personally and individually. It's the Jesus who calls us to be disciples, to be compassionate, to go to the marginalized and the least. It's the Jesus who opens up the deepest realities of life, modeling what it means to truly live, to completely love, and to be genuinely free. It's the Jesus who comes so that we might have life and have it more abundantly (Jn 10:10).

All of us—young people and adults—are yearning for this fullness of life. Sometimes we can so rationalize Jesus, set him so far apart from us, so distant from us, that we don't feel we can follow because his Good News doesn't apply to us. We can so emphasize his divinity that he doesn't speak to our humanity. The Good News is okay for Jesus, but what can you expect from mere humans or mere young people?

It's time to call young people to the whole Gospel, the challenging and transforming aspect of the Gospel, the entire Good News.

Yes, some of our young people are hurting, overwhelmed, and in need of compassion and healing. But some youth want more, are ready for more! They want the Gospel that transforms, the faith that does justice, changes lives, and changes society.

Sometimes we hold back because we think they are not ready—and sometimes we hold back because we are not ready. When young people look at the Church as institution, parish, or individual ministers and members, do they see something that would make them want to have "our" faith? do they see a noble calling and affirmative, optimistic religious conviction? Do they see the fullness of life and the reign of God? We must proclaim clearly: "The darkness doesn't win! Death doesn't win! Violence doesn't win! Injustice doesn't win! Crucifixion doesn't win!"

This is the Christmas message: that light comes into the world. This is the Easter Message: that resurrection overcomes crucifixion. Many young people have known fears, violence, abuse, or addiction. They need to hear the Good News that the darkness doesn't win!

We, too, are on a journey. We experience pain, death, loneliness, brokenness, woundedness, unjust or unresponsive church and societal structures, but the darkness doesn't win! We need to hear the Good News too!

Has this Good News ever been proclaimed to young people? Have they been moved? Are they more joyful, compassionate, loving, peaceful, and courageous? Are they connected to the community of believers? Have they been challenged by Jesus' call to discipleship?

George Gallup describes our young people as perhaps the most spiritual generation we have ever seen in our Church. He writes, "The challenge to the churches is to build up their youth programs and put young people in places where they can challenge, disagree, and build up trust. If the world in the next century is going to be less sexist, less racist, less polluted, and more peaceful, we can thank our young people."[3]

If our Church in this new century is going to be more inclusive, more creative in our prayer and worship, more committed to justice and service, more centered on the Eucharist, and guided by committed and competent ordained and lay ministers, we can thank our young people.

As our opening scripture reading asserted: How wonderful is the coming of those who bring Good News!

---

1 George H. Gallup, Jr. *Religion in America 1996* (Princeton Religion Research Center, 1996), 24.

2 Craig Kennet Miller, *Postmoderns: The Beliefs, Hopes & Fears of Young Americans, 1965-1981* (Nashville: Discipleship Resources, 1996).

3 George Gallup, Jr. and D. Michael Lindsay, *Surveying the Religious Landscape: Trends in U.S. Beliefs* (Harrisburg: Morehouse Publishing, 1999). Quoted in *The Dallas Morning News*, December 12, 1999.

# REFLECTION QUESTIONS

How would you describe an evangelized person? How open are you to being evangelized by the young people to whom you minister?

How can we more intentionally proclaim the name of Jesus in our ministry? Do we believe that the Gospel has power and can attract the youth of today? How can we act on this belief?

What are the major challenges to effective youth evangelization? What kind of programs, activities, and events have a positive impact on youth evangelization?

---

**Robert McCarty** *is the executive director for the National Federation for Catholic Youth Ministry, which provides networking, resources, and leadership for the development of youth ministry within the Catholic Church. He has been in professional youth ministry since 1973, serving in diocesan, parish, school, and community programs. He has a B.S. in sociology and theology from St. Joseph's University in Philadelphia, an M.A. in religious education from LaSalle University in Philadelphia, and a doctorate of ministry from the Graduate Theological Foundation in Indiana. He offers workshops and training programs in youth ministry skills and issues internationally.*

# Catholic Youth Evangelization:
# A Method to the Madness!

## 1. Characteristics of the Millennial Generation
- They are believers, though not necessarily belongers
- They are spiritual, though not necessarily religious
- They emphasize the individual spiritual journey, not the communal tradition
- They desire a genuine experience of the transcendence of God
- They desire a faith that provides meaning and purpose, that makes sense
- They relate to a Jesus who understands suffering
- They want to grow in faith together with peers and adults
- Everything expresses the transcendent: nature, the arts, gatherings, devotionals

## 2. New questions for our ministry . . . Will our faith have children?
- How do we proclaim the Good News in a language young people understand?
- How do we connect young people to the faith community and to its mission?
- How do we call young people to be disciples and followers of Jesus?

## 3. Key factors in our efforts: witnesses and storytellers
- The Church as institution
- The faith community
- The individual minister

## 4. A Process for Evangelization
- Contact
  — Be where young people are
  — Be known to young people
  — Encourage young people to become "inviters"
  — Go to young people when they can't come to us

- Connect
  — Develop personal relationships
  — Involve young people in the faith community
  — Connect young people with Jesus
- Commitment
  — Personal decision and journey
  — Call to discipleship

## 5. Challenges
- Proclaim the Good News, and proclaim it again
- Connect young people to the life of the faith community
- Challenge young people to be disciples to a noble adventure
- Give young people the opportunity to serve
- Create a faith community where the Jesus dream is realized

# Catholic Youth Evangelization: A Self-Assessment

*Using the dynamics of Catholic youth evangelization, assess your current evangelization efforts:*

## Dynamic #1: WITNESS
- What opportunities exist for youth to interact with adults who are living out their faith?
- What opportunities exist for young people to share how they live out their faith?
- What opportunities exist for youth to hear from adults about the challenge of living out their faith?
- What practical strategies could be utilized to foster this interaction and sharing by adults and youth?

## Dynamic #2: OUTREACH
- Where do young people in our parish or community spend their time?
- Where can adults in youth ministry spend time to build relationships with young people?
- How can our adults become better known to the young people of our parish?

- How does our ministry impact or reach out to the families of our young people?
- What settings for young people require that the Church go to them, because they can't come to us?
- What practical strategies could be utilized to build relationships of trust, acceptance and caring?

### Dynamic #3: PROCLAMATION

- Where do young people explicitly hear the Good News?
- Where is the Jesus story told?
- What opportunities exist for young people to discuss and share the Good News of Jesus?
- What practical strategies could infuse the Good News into existing events, activities and gatherings?
- What practical approaches would enable our young people to really 'hear' the Good News in a language that they understand?

## Dynamic #4: INVITATION

- How are young people currently invited into the Church, its organizations and its life?
- What is it like for a young person to attend our Sunday liturgy? How are they welcomed?
- How are young people invited to participate in liturgy?
- How is the participation of young people fostered in the life of our parish?
- How is our sense of hospitality extended to young people?
- What practical strategies could be utilized to invite young people to more full participation in our Church?

## Dynamic #5: CONVERSION

- How are young people invited into a deeper relationship with Jesus and the community?
- Where do young people hear of the ongoing decision to be open to God's presence in their lives?
- How are young people led into a full maturing of faith?
- Where do young people discuss those factors leading away from a relationship with Jesus? Discuss those factors leading towards a relationship with Jesus.
- What practical strategies could be utilized to foster youths' growth in faith?

## Dynamic #6: DISCIPLESHIP

- Where do young people hear the call to live as followers of Jesus?
- Where do young people hear, discuss and share the challenge of daily living as disciples?
- Where do young people learn the "skills" for discipleship?
- What opportunities exist for young people to participate in the building of the Reign of God?
- What practical strategies would foster the participation of young people in justice and service activities?

# General Session

## BEYOND SAFE SPACE: EVANGELIZING YOUNG ADULTS

Michelle Miller and Brett Hoover, CSP

The vast majority of young adults are occasionally church-going or non-practicing but spiritually-oriented and believing people. To reach out to them and speak to their considerable spiritual needs in the contemporary world, we need to move beyond the "comfort zone" of our usual church spaces and ways of doing things. We have to look for ways of celebrating new and old "sacramental" moments of connection and transformation with the Catholic community; new ways of encouraging belonging and commitment; rituals old and new to speak to generations in search of transcendence; and new ways of forming young people as true adults in the faith.

Our charge today is to tackle the call to evangelize young adults. That "e" word alone would have many young adults already confused, to say nothing for most of the other Catholics in our great country. We were initially excited about our presentation because be both feel passionately about young adults and their place in the church, and their call to be disciples of Jesus. But we were challenged in our preparation because we are not here to offer you a magic solution, and we assume that is what many of you are praying or begging for.

We do not have the program to engage the young adults in your communities. But we are hoping to invite you to think differently as to who these young adult are, how they came to be such interesting and challenging members of our faith community, and how you are going to journey with them in living out the Gospel of Jesus Christ. If you take anything away from our presentation, we hope that you will be inspired to go home and ask the young adults in your community this simple question: "What is it like to be you, and how can this faith community be a part of your journey to God?"

By a slim margin, Brett and I are teetering on the upper cusp of the young adult age range. We have shared with one another that it will be a sad day when we are no longer welcomed at a church meeting by a greeting like, "It is so nice to have such young people involved!" We admit we have often groaned to ourselves at such salutations, but we humbly admit that future such greetings are truly numbered.

## Who Are Young Adults?

We'd like to start out by clarifying to whom we refer when we are using the term "young adult." The bishops of the United States in their publication *Sons and Daughters of the Light: A Pastoral Plan for Ministry with Young Adults* define young adults as those in their late teens, twenties, and thirties. We do understand that in some areas of North America and in various cultures and communities in the States, that ministry to younger Catholics may take on different age ranges. For instance, in many Latino communities, ministry to younger Catholics, or *jovenes*, may refer to those not married who are sixteen to twenty-five or so. For the sake of consistency in our presentation, we will generally refer to young adult Catholics as those post-high school up through those in their thirties, both single and married, with or without children; in other words, using the bishops' definition of those in their late teens, twenties, and thirties.[1]

It also helps to clarify that we very cautiously make generalizations of such a huge age and developmental range. A nineteen-year-old is in a different place then someone who is twenty-seven, who is different than someone who is thirty-five. So again, we invite you to get to know your own communities of young adults and find out who they really are. Our presentation is meant to animate the vastness of the current Catholic young adults, not to explain them in definitive terms.

So who are young adults and what makes this current generation different? The present population of young adult Catholics were mostly born between 1968 and 1985. Current research estimates that there are approximately twenty-five million young adult Catholics out of a total Catholic population of around sixty-three million. This would make young adult Catholics at least forty percent of our total population.[2]

One fascinating aspect of the present population of young adult Catholics is that they have been raised mostly by baby-boomer parents. These boomers straddled the event of the Second Vatican Council and the ensuing transformation of the Church. These baby-boomers grew up in one Church and raised their children in another. Many of these boomers have had to renegotiate their own relationship with the Church in light of Vatican II. Some would say that they are still trying to figure out what happened and where they fit.

These parents and their unique faith journeys have had a significant impact on how they raised their children in the faith. This may be helpful to keep in mind as we continue to explore young adult Catholics today. Rude awakening for the day: half of those young adults in a recent survey had never heard of the Second Vatican Council. Suffice to say, Vatican II is no longer the frame of reference for the majority of Catholics in the United States (Hoge, 59-60).

> **Challenge for Evangelizers:** How does my own experience of Vatican II influence my thoughts and motives as a Catholic? Is this influence assisting or inhibiting my evangelization of young adults?

It will come as no surprise to you that the current population of young adults is amazingly diverse in many ways, especially ethnically and culturally. According to the Center for Applied Research in the Apostolate (CARA) those Catholics in the United States who were born before 1943 are about 88 percent white, nine percent Hispanic, two percent black or African American, and one percent Asian. The Catholic population born between 1961 and 1982 is 70 percent white, 23 percent Hispanic, three percent black or African American, three percent Asian, and one percent

Native American. Most every ethnic group, except those identified as white, is increasing within the Catholic community.[3]

**Challenge for Evangelizers:** Do our evangelization efforts and strategies honestly and effectively take this blossoming cultural reality into account?

So what about all we hear of young adults and their disinterest in the Church? The good news is that many young adults do value being Catholic. The research team of Hoge, Dinges, Johnson, and Gonzales found that about 90 percent of the young adults surveyed continue to check the "Catholic" box and cannot imagine being anything else! (Hoge, 45) This is indeed the good news. The challenge comes when we look beyond casual or cultural affiliation into community participation and the impact Catholicity has on their everyday lives.

The CARA research points out that 37 percent of pre-Vatican II Catholics born before 1943 reported that their Catholic faith was the most important thing in their lives. Only 14 percent of post-Vatican II Catholics born after 1960 said the same. But what Brett and I find interesting is that 41 of these post-Vatican II Catholics stated that their Catholic faith was important to them, and "so are many other areas." This seems to be very characteristic of current Catholic young adults. They are energized, challenged, and nourished spiritually, intellectually, and socially by a huge variety of arenas. The neighborhood Catholic parish is no longer the center of their world as it was for some past generations. The global world, figuratively and actually, is their center.

**Challenge for Evangelizers:** Am I frustrated or inspired by young adults and their unique reality?

Having said this, we also note that the majority of those in the United States believe in God and most feel comfortable saying so. But a lot of people also talk of feeling uncomfortable describing that relationship in terms of the language of religion. "Religion" often automatically makes people think of institutions. The term "spirituality" makes people think of relationship, of faith, of God.[4] That may be a bit strange to most of us in the Church business. Did you know at least one survey reported that people have a more positive attitude toward the military than they do toward the Church?[5]

The good news is that people seem to be less and less anti-religious than they used to, even if they don't articulate organized religion in relationship to their own personal faith. In other words, religion doesn't seem evil or wrong to a lot of people; it just seems sort of quaint or irrelevant.[6]

So what about young adults and their sense of allegiance or obligation? According to the Hoge research, young adults, as well as many other Americans, have no sense of owing loyalty to any institution as such. Institutions have to earn this loyalty. And in a world where young adults are seen by many as nothing but a consumer commodity, it's no wonder! (Hoge, 221)

Imagine young adults walking in authenticity armor. To break through this armor, there must be validation through experience and the experience of authenticity. And most young adults are not alienated or angry like some baby-boomer Catholics; to be angry, one must be invested. Hoge and colleagues note that many young adult Catholics merely live a self-defined Catholicism that takes into account their global reality.

They embrace those values, experiences, and traditions of the Church that aid their own navigation through life. This is how they live. They have been taught to choose what works, what inspires, what brings value to their lives. Most have no concept needing to embrace every and all aspects of Catholicism, that just wouldn't make any sense, unless, of course, all of these aspects came with authentic and life-giving explanations of how they lead us to God (Hoge, 224-227).

This kind of philosophy is a challenge to any institution that has lost its ability or interest to make grounded and authentic explanations a part of its own existence. Our Church has a long-standing tradition of promoting the idea of obligation. But let's face it, we have not always followed that up with a teaching based in love and the Gospel of Jesus. "Because the Church says so," will not cut it with these young folks.

> **Challenge for Evangelizers:** How are we going to model and share the concept of obligation as an authentic and life-giving response to God, ourselves, and others?

Before we go any further, we would like to address the myth that there is a huge rush of young adults who are running towards and grasping onto what is commonly labeled Catholic Orthodoxy. This is simply not the case. We think it's important to note that those young adults who find their spirituality in such movements make up a small minority of young adults. There is another minority group of young adults who are comfortable with the Church's reforms and are actively involved in the parish and the Catholic faith community in the United States. But make no mistake, the vast majority of young adult Catholics are not engaged in the life of the Catholic faith community. This is our challenge and opportunity.[7]

Young adults are products of society, culture, church, family, and friends. And if by their very current lived experiences they are a challenge to the Church as we know it, then we had better get to work.

The Gospel of Jesus Christ is timeless and for all generations. So it is up to us to meet young adults where they are and to invite them into an authentic relationship with God and with the Catholic faith community. We are not saying that this invitation is void of accountability, responsibility, or challenge. We are saying that the invitation itself is what seems to be lacking in many communities. This is not rocket science; it is just living as Jesus would. The task of inviting young adults into community should be nothing but an honor.

## What the Church Offers

Given all the challenges facing young adults in the world they are a part of, what does the Catholic community have to offer them and what gifts do young adults bring to the Church?

## 1. The Catholic Church Offers a Relationship with Jesus Christ

My mother would most likely explain that she found a relationship with Christ through her relationship with the Catholic Church. I, on the other hand, feel as though I found a relationship with the Church through my relationship with Jesus Christ. A personal relationship with God in Christ is the foundation to life in the Church, but it may come about in a variety of ways.

We've already talked of young adults and their experience of being spiritual but not religious. Many young adults may know God outside the Catholic faith community, or any organized religion for that matter. And the Church offers such an important foundation! A life authentically centered on Jesus is attractive. Is our Catholic witness Christ-centered or Church-centered? Unfortunately, the two are not always interchangeable.

## 2. The Catholic Church Offers an Amazingly Rich Tradition

This one may be a little trickier. We just noted the idea that many young adults would say that they are spiritual and yet not engaged in the Catholic Church. But the more we understand why we do what we do as Catholics, the more we can begin to embrace the uniqueness of our Catholic faith and the wholeness our tradition can bring to our lives. Young adults may know when to sit and stand and kneel at Mass, but have we ever really talked about why we change our postures during the Liturgy? Why does the Church take a stand on moral and social issues, from abortion and premarital sex to poverty and the minimum wage? And we have such wonderful resources to share these explanations! I am not taking about the memorization that my own mother is still proud of from her years as a Catholic; I mean really knowing why we do what we do as Catholics. Our Church has an amazingly rich tapestry of things that feed the soul. We so beautifully commemorate life through the Church. Our tradition has the potential to enliven all our senses as we search for real depth in the midst of our longings and hungers!

We have rich and authentic ways to explain and share our traditions; we just need to find appropriate and engaging ways to make sure we do this with authenticity and love. When did passing on the Faith become a chore and not a blessing? When did questioning become irritating and not inspiring? If young adults challenge the Church to define who we are and how we are called to engage the world as disciples of Jesus, then so be it. Grace is found in the midst of appropriating our faith.

### 3. The Catholic Church Offers an Outwardly Focused, External View of the World

In a culture that is often bent on self-obsession, our faith demands that we live for others. This philosophy can be a breath of fresh air to young adults who discover at some point that there is more to life than only their own happiness. Studies show young adults are drawn to service for others. They see a connection between their faith and the call to lighten the burdens of others. CARA reported that after following their consciences, helping the needy was the most important aspect of the Catholic faith for surveyed young adults. This is great news. We all say at some point, "Is this all there is?" And our Catholic Tradition says, "No! There is more! Get out and do something for someone else!"

### 4. The Catholic Church Offers a Community of the Faithful

The concept of community is rapidly changing in our global world, but when you ask young adults what they are looking for within the Church, they often state that they are looking for a sense of belonging and community. Ask young adults why they attend a particular parish and we think many will tell you it is there they feel welcome and part of the community. In a world that often offers hollow experiences of intimacy, providing opportunities for young adults to engage with, and draw energy from, others on this journey of faith is priceless. Parishes are made for people, not the other way around! Mobility, individualism, and consumerism often keep us busy enough that community is hard to find. But community is all about people! And the Church needs to be about finding new ways to create and engage in community-building. Young adults may remark that meeting other Catholic people of their age is what gives them hope and energy for their own journeys of faith. Jesus never meant for us to go it alone.

We have shared what we think the Church has to offer. What do young adults have to offer the Church? Their very presence. And from that, we will glean the riches that they bring, the unique face of Jesus that is theirs alone. Let us be attentive to their gifts, and walk with them on this path to Jesus.

How do we do this? Well, Brett has the challenge to present more of the disconnect between Church and young adults and how to bridge the gap.

# Bridging the Gap

How do we walk with young adults?

This is one of those questions where I imagine Jesus standing in front of us saying, "Wake up, Church!"

I don't want to be ambiguous about this at all; we believe that the situation of young adults in the Church has become a crisis. The disconnect between the world of young adults and the world of the Church has become a chasm.

But every crisis is an opportunity. Many Catholic parishes, campus ministries, colleges, and other groups are effectively reaching out to Catholic young adults, packing them into the Liturgy, bringing them to RCIA programs, making a reputation in their communities as lively places where all are welcome and the Spirit is making a difference in people's lives. These places are bridging the gap.

We'd like to talk about the strategies employed by successful ministries, plus some dreams of our own about how to bridge the gap.

## A. Sacramental Moments

Thinking specifically of the first goal of *Go and Make Disciples* and of *Sons and Daughters of the Light*, which is connecting young adults with God in Jesus Christ, Michelle and I strongly believe that as evangelizers in the community of the Church, we can and ought to be present for young adults at sacramental moments.[8] We should be instruments of the Spirit, to help them articulate and find God's light in their experience at those key life moments when young people are open to encountering the Mystery of God. We know, as *Evangelii Nuntiandi* reminds us, the light is already there in the experience of young people. I think with young

adults, as with any underrepresented group, there's a danger of "We have the Gospel, they need it," in our approach. [9]

I'd like to say a few things about some specific sacramental moments:

*Weddings and Baptisms—the Capital "S" Sacraments*

Most of you have heard this before. But we strongly remind everyone of the ill-advised philosophy of "coerced hoop-jumping" that requires young people to be registered members of a parish before we even talk to them about getting married or baptizing their children. Most young adults, with their lack of knowledge of the Church world, probably don't really know what it means to be registered and may just assume we are throwing bureaucracy in their way like every other institution. It is good to challenge people to commitment, but I think by requiring registration, we are in a sense exalting our administrative procedures over the theology of Baptism. These young people are baptized Catholics who desire the Sacraments. Our first response to them should be to find out what their stories are, especially their spiritual stories. Our call is to engage them on that level first.

One of the questions I ask and encourage others to ask young adults in pre-Cana is: "Do you believe God brought you together?" That's often a shocker for people—they are not used to that language. But it always leads to a conversation. Or with Baptism: "How has this child of yours been a gift from God? Why would you want him or her to be part of a faith community?"

This is a generation with a strong spiritual interest, but whose members often don't equate the institutional Church with things spiritual. Our job is to change that reputation. We need to put the Sacraments in spiritual terms, both in preparation programs and in the Wedding and Baptism homilies, which are unparalleled opportunities to talk to hordes of young adults and show them a vibrant and relevant Church.

### Small "S" Sacramental Moments

Aside from the official sacraments, there are all those key moments in human life when young adults are open to mystery, when they realize they are not in control, when young adults get hit by the 2x4 of Christ. This is when their sense of dependency and vulnerability becomes obvious.

From an evangelization point of view, this is a time when we in the Church community can be there with young adults—not to take control but to listen and help them see that God is present.

A lot of the small "s" sacramental moments I am thinking of are those that people would not generally associate with going to church. In fact, church might be the last place they might think these moments should show up. But the truth is, these are times when people's lives have entered an extremely vulnerable state, when they need support and help, when they need to see the presence of God in the middle of the darkness. In other words, it's the experience of the cross: life as these young adults did not expect it and may not understand.

Divorce is a more and more common experience of this sort among young people. Maybe you have heard the term "starter marriage," a somewhat pejorative term for the phenomenon of marriages between young people that last only a couple of years and never really develop a mature sense of commitment. It's easy to lament what this term says about society, but we forget that when we speak from the pulpit or train ministers to deal with young adults, we are ultimately dealing with individual people who may be feeling very badly that they have failed at love. If they are Catholic, they are probably thinking, "This wasn't supposed to happen to me." What they need from us rather than blame are ears to listen to their story as a story of faith. Who else is going to suggest to them that in the experience of failure and pain, God is present, that in the midst of their very failure of love they might find redemption? That is the wisdom of the cross. That would be a Christian message.

We might also ask the question of how pastoral our annulment process is, since that is the first place many divorced young people encounter the Church, and that is the first place they are likely to tell their stories as stories of faith. And we're not talking about watering down our tradition on marriage here, but placing our pastoral relationship first and foremost. That's just humane.

Another complex issue but one that also deserves our attention: can the Church be a place where young men and women go when they are facing up to a homosexual orientation? Based on our observations, many young people find this a very difficult situation, in which they expect condemnation from others and sometimes find self-hatred in their own hearts. Before we even try to approach the complexities of the Church's teaching, can we just give these young people a place to tell their stories as stories of faith and assure them that God is present even in the darkest of days?

Another very common young adult experience is that of returning from prison. The latest statistics show us that over two million people are in prison in the United States, the highest number of any country on earth—and a huge number of those are young adults. We know that prison ministry is often understaffed and underfunded, and that it is an extremely challenging ministry for those who do take it on, either as chaplains or as volunteers. We have personally witnessed how recidivism is an incredible temptation for young adults who return to their old neighborhoods—back to old friends and old patterns. But a return could also be a moment of grace, especially if people know that the church is a place they can go when they come home, where someone in the parish will hear their story as a story of faith, where on that first Sunday back there is a welcoming and unconditional blessing for them.

That last point makes me wonder why we can't ritualize the frequent comings and goings of all our young adults in this extremely mobile society. When I was leaving for the seminary, the parish I belonged to gave me a sending blessing. Why should such things only be reserved for would-be seminarians? In a way, that's discrimination. Why not bless those leaving for military service, for a university education, for volunteer work, for a move to another city for a job or to be with someone they love? And what about blessing those who have just arrived? Wouldn't recent immigrants and newcomers to town be marvelously surprised if

*" The pastoral care of young adults demands*
*a certain kind of openness and flexibility.*
*Parish leaders need an awareness of the life*
*patterns, transience, and mobility of young adults.*
*Those who work with young adults will need an*
*approach that is nonjudgmental yet challenging. "*

*Sons and Daughters of the Light:*
*A Pastoral Plan for Ministry With Young Adults*
(Part 3: "A Plan for Ministry")

we had a blessing once a month for everyone who had arrived within the last four weeks?

## B. Belonging and Commitment

If we are anxious for young adults to belong to our Church community, we have to take a serious look at how we commonly talk about belonging to the Church, because I don't think it's "young adult friendly" at all. For example, how do we generally define membership in a faith community? In terms of families. How many families does your parish have? This is interesting, considering that statistically speaking the age for marriage and parenting is moving up across ethnic groups in this country. In other words, we have a system designed to exclude a large number of our young unmarried adults.[10]

Another questionable area is participation in ministries. Many lay ministers are people who have been faithfully serving the Church since Vatican II. By now, most of these people have fairly stable lives and consistent participation. Many young adults have neither. Most young people will not be Eucharistic ministers three weeks in a row. If someone makes reference in the announcements to what was said last week at Mass, the young people won't understand because many weren't there.

You see the problem. Over time, the Church lay apostolate has unknowingly built an "in" club that does not encourage the involvement of young people. Can we find other ways of doing these things?

I once served in an urban parish loaded with young adults, where registration was done every fall over several Sundays on a card with more than just the nuclear family as a set of options. Announcements were repeated week after week, since it was understood many people didn't attend weekly. And, believe me, no one was ever scheduled three weeks in a row for any ministry.

Aside from these basic challenges to us church folk as to how to think about belonging for young adults, there are other questions that I think we need to keep in mind as well. I'd like to raise one in particular that some of my colleagues and I agree doesn't get talked about enough.

Among all young adults, one of the most underrepresented groups in the Church is the so-called Second Generation (2G)—the young adult children of first-generation immigrants. The 2Gs may not identify with the Church of their parents, nor are they always grateful for how the Church bridged the gap between their countries of origin and the United States. They could care less. They were born here and know how to get along just fine, thank you.[11]

The 2Gs belong to what some scholars call a hybrid culture: they are U.S. American and they are also Latin American, to use one common example. But they also often feel in a sense like they are neither. They are betwixt and between. They are "bridge people," but we often haven't really appreciated that in the Church nor found a place for their gifts to shine. We need to engage them more and ask about their spiritual stories.

Some of the experiences of "bridge people" will be the same as other young adults, but some of it will be unique. This is another huge group of young adults that—from anecdotal evidence anyway—is lapsed in practice but loyal in self-affiliation (Hoge, 117-119).

*Commitment*

Evangelization, of course, is about every one of us moving into the depths of a relationship with the Mystery of God in Jesus. We hope that belonging to a community of faith is a part of deepening that relationship as well as motivating us to be a part of God's transformation of the world around us. If not, we might as well all go to work teaching school or doing social work; at least we'd know we were getting something decent done.

Of course, our faith calls us all to move to a deeper level of commitment. Yet that seems to be exactly the greatest challenge for young adults in a world of ever greater mobility, of low employer-employee loyalty, of frightening divorce statistics, of consumerism, of ever-disposable products. Not to mention that young adulthood itself, for a large number of young people in the United States, is a kind of in-between zone, where they may be financially independent but haven't taken on all the responsibilities of family or leadership in church or society. So, as we say in our generation, commitment might be an issue.

That's why smaller commitments are often so much more successful with young adults. The conventional wisdom used to be that young adults wouldn't get involved with social justice. Now after the anti-sweatshop movement and the anti-war movement, people are thinking twice about saying that. But the way to get young adults involved is to ask for commitments that will work with their highly transitional and mobile lives.

Try asking for discrete commitments: "I need you from this time to this time on this day. Can you do that?" That's why Theology on Tap and spring break volunteer trips work well, but weekly soup kitchen commitments can be a challenge.

Some young adults will commit still more of their time and energy, and most of us know that. Leadership development is always an aim in young adult ministry. Anyone who isn't constantly thinking about leadership development isn't doing young adult ministry.

Your leaders are the ones among whom to develop a culture of outreach and hospitality. They are the ones you spend your time on, carefully developing the attitude that our job is to make sure that no one is ever ungreeted and unwelcomed.

Never undersell young adults. Often times, a challenge is exactly what they will appreciate. That is one of the points of Colleen Carroll's book *The New Faithful*.[12] People adore romantic gestures and heroic challenges. Sometimes we don't get much out of young people because we don't ask much of them, or because we only ask it in the same tired old terms like, "Come to Mass every Sunday." Yeah, that's heroic.

What about: "Make as much of a financial commitment to helping Catholic Charities assist the poor as you do to keeping your body in shape at the gym?" "Raise $2,000 for orphans in Nicaragua and then come down to Managua to build for them." "What are you willing to do for your soul, your spirit? Would you like to try spiritual reading twenty minutes every day, a silent retreat for a weekend?" Everyone loves a challenge.

*Rituals New and Old*

Young people are spiritually hungry. That's almost become a cliché, but it's true, and our Catholic sacramental life provides some amazing resources to address this. We also know that it is the deep experience of prayer and ritual that fires people up to work for the transformation of their own lives and of the world around them.

But prayer isn't easy in our culture. We are always wrestling with that couch-potato tendency toward passivity that comes to us from our world of entertainment, and that I think enters into our churches. We watch; we don't participate. Ironically, on the other end, we are fighting with an American cultural tendency toward wanting to be in control all the time. Let's face it: ritual and prayer work because, within a structure, we finally learn to let go.

If most young people have any experience of ritual and prayer, it's going to happen at the Sunday liturgy. I'm not a liturgist and I don't pretend to be. But I know those celebrations need to be vital—prayerful and alive. Our preaching has to be a living thing.

First of all, it has to be in plain English. Too many homilies are done in a religious language impenetrable to today's young adults. (In fact, older adults don't like it either—I went to mass with my seventy-year-old aunt in her parish in a small town in north central Indiana. The young priest gave the homily, speaking about everyday things. My aunt turned to me helplessly and said, "See now, I understand what he's talking about.")

I hate to criticize priests about this. We've had a hard year and a half. A lot of us were specifically trained to talk in religious gibberish so that it would sound exalted and holy. And often as priests the way we live can be so different from that of everybody else that it's easy to lose track of what everyday examples and issues really are. The rest of you, gently teach us how to speak English again. Remind us to be imaginative.

## Music

Again, this element must be vital and energetic. Young adults don't necessarily all like the same kinds of music. Different kinds will play better in different geographic locations, in different cultural groups, maybe even at different Masses. That's okay, as long as it's alive.

If we should actually get people to attend church beyond the Sunday Liturgy, they may be interested in some of the wonderful ritual opportunities that we offer as Catholics. You have no doubt heard that Eucharistic Adoration has become popular again among certain groups of young people. Why should this surprise us? Done well, it's a feast for the senses—candles, darkness, a strong visual element, silence. Where else do young adults have silence in their lives?

There is also a definitely Catholic identity issue in this ceremony, for a group that sometimes feels awash in a world of confusion. Eucharistic Adoration is the vestige of an old world where it identities seemed stronger and more anchored, where people knew who they were. Participating in Eucharistic Adoration is the experience of becoming part of something larger than oneself, a tradition that seems almost timeless.

We shouldn't also overlook the potential for other prayer and ritual experiences beyond this. We've got them, and from Morning and Evening Prayer, to Taize, to new rituals like the Veneration of the Word that occur on Paulist National Catholic Evangelization Association Missions, to a mix like the Tenebrae services we used to do at Cal Berkeley during Holy Week, these ceremonies are a little ancient and a little modern.

The power of retreat experiences should not be forgotten. Many young adults are familiar with this idea from high school or childhood, or have at least heard of them. Charis Ministries in Chicago offers day-long, weekend, and twelve-step oriented experiences to many young adults. At the website *BustedHalo.com*, we are testing an online retreat in cooperation with Charis, in the hope that we might use it with young adults.

### Formation of True Adults in the Faith

While in a sense the formation of young adults in the Faith is a separate question from evangelization, it's important to note that the young adults we are talking about are coming from a world pretty much without religious roots of any depth. At one time, people could assume that American young adults would be raised with a certain basic knowledge of Judeo-Christian religion. For those born as Catholics, there would be a basic knowledge of that culture, bred by family, parish, and community.

That world no longer exists, and young adults' knowledge of their faith traditions can almost never be underestimated. In the evangelization of young adults the dictum must be, as Father John Cusick of Chicago says, "Assume little, explain lots." [13]

On the other hand, it's important to note how curious about faith and religion young adults are. They want to overcome their lack of knowledge, but are often reluctant to admit their lack of instruction and ask for help. Thus, any opportunities we can create to provide information in a non-threatening atmosphere can become the evangelizing *coup d'etat*.

The Internet can work particularly well in this regard. Many campus ministries and some young-adult-friendly parishes have developed web-based question-and-answer services for young adults. We do it nationally at *BustedHalo.com*, the young adult spirituality web site that I run. At *BustedHalo.com*, we also provide an extensive section with information on the Mass, the Bible (called Bible Boot Camp), prayer, and various aspects of Catholic Tradition. It's topped off by a spiritual trivia game called Dante's Trivia Inferno. If you answer the questions right you travel on the elevator up to heaven. If you lose, well, your entrance to hell is accompanied by a blood-curdling scream.

The point is, we need many different places and methods for delivering the background information about spirituality that young adults are missing, and if it's easy and fun to access, it may provide an "in" for evangelization, the beginning of a conversation. On our website, young adults also find a discussion board, a kind of online community, and something called a *Church Search*, offering the names and locations of actual communities that have been recommended by other young adults all over the United States and Canada.

We recognize that information on the Internet is not a substitute for real interpersonal contact. What we are talking about here is creating a multi-layered matrix of institutions and methods to bridge the education gap. There's a diocese-wide Bible study program for Catholic college students in Arkansas that uses our website in tandem with its materials.

I know I'm making it sound like it's always about the Internet, but communicating could be as simple as examining a theme of Catholic social teaching in Sunday homilies and then have it reinforced in a colorful handout distributed after mass or a PowerPoint presentation after communion. People learn in different ways, so we want to approach them from a number of angles, especially in our very audio-visual culture.

# Conclusion

As Michelle and I have been eager to communicate, we don't believe there is one program or one answer to evangelizing young adults in the globalized world of today. As a matter of fact, it's probably true to say that no one knows exactly how to do it. This is fluid ministry that is often messy. It demands presence at various levels.

What we've tried to offer here is a change in our way of thinking about ministering to young adults, along with some suggestions of how we might reach out a little differently. I know it probably sounds like we're inviting you to listen to the whole world's personal faith stories, and I know all of you don't have time. But we figure some of you out there do—peer ministers, parish hospitality teams, young adult leaders, parish staff.

Some things we know are working, and other ideas we see show promise. Beyond that, we just keep trying things to see what works.

Mike Hayes, who works with me in Paulist Young Adult Ministries, will try just about anything, and I know Michelle and I feel the same way. We'll stand on our heads, jump up and down, say silly things to an audience of people from all over North and South America, just to get the Church's attention about this important group in its midst, and to get young adults' attention about the riches of the mystery of God in Christ.

We were saying earlier how Baptism has got to supercede parish registration in terms of how we reach out. If we really believe that, then the fact that so many of our young adults (who make up about 40 percent of our Catholic community) are missing, leads us to feel that we are not complete as a community of faith, as a Church.

Young adults bring challenges, yes, but they also bring energy, vitality, and the call for authenticity. They are one of the groups that keep us focused on mission instead of maintenance.

So like the father in the story of the prodigal son, let us hear, validate, and learn from those who have been persistent enough to stick it out, and let us run out to meet those young adults who wait in the distance for an invitation home.

1  *Sons and Daughters of the Light: A Pastoral Plan for Ministry With Young Adults* (Washington, DC: USCCB, 1996), iv.

2  William D. Dinges, Mary Johnson, and Juan L. Gonzalez, Jr., *Young Adult Catholics: Religion in the Culture of Choice*, ed. Dean R. Hoge (Notre Dame: University of Notre Dame Press, 2001), 13-18.

3  The Center for Applied Research in the Apostolate (CARA), *Special Report–Young Adult Catholics* (Fall 2002), 2.

4  Humphrey Taylor, *The Religious and Other Beliefs of Americans, 2003*. The Harris Poll #11, (February 26, 2003).

5  Robin Toner, "Trust in the Military Heightens Among Baby Boomers' Children," *The New York Times* (May 23, 2003), Sec. A:1.

6  The observation about people being less anti-religious was made by Fr. John Cusick of Chicago, based on more than twenty-five years in young adult ministry. See also Hoge, et al.

7  *The Search for Common Ground: What Unites and Divides Catholic Americans*, ed. (Huntington, IN: Our Sunday Visitor, 1997), 126-131. Only 2 percent of young adults said that premarital sex is always wrong. Only eleven percent thought one should obey Church teachings even if they are not understood, and only 30 percent believed that the Catholic Church was the One True Church. This does not sounds like a generation moving toward majority membership in the new orthodoxy movement. In Hoge et al., Catholics involved in their parishes made up only eight to nine percent of the sample. A majority of these, 69-79 percent, depending on ethnicity, held a traditional sense of doctrine, but 33-39 percent believed one could be a good Catholic without attending Mass at all. These do not sound like the beliefs of people devoted to doctrinal clarity.

8  United States Conference of Catholic Bishops, *Go and Make Disciples: Tenth Anniversary Spanish and English Edition* (Washington, DC: USCCB, 2002).

9  Pope Paul VI, *Evangelii Nuntiandi: On Evangelization in the Modern World* (Washington, DC: USCCB, 1975).

10  National Center for Health Statistics, *Advance Report of Final Marriage Statistics, 1989 and 1990* (Centers for Disease Control and Prevention, 2002)

11  These characteristics are based on the authors' observations from years in youth ministry and from conversations with second-generation theologians and lay ministers.

12  Colleen Carroll, *The New Faithful: Why Young Adults Are Embracing Christian Orthodoxy* (Chicago: Loyola Press, 2002).

13  John Cusick, Katherine F. Devries, and Wilton D. Gregory, *The Basic Guide to Young Adult Ministry* (Phoenix: Orbis, 2001), 121.

# REFLECTION QUESTIONS

In what ways can we get past the negative connotations that young adults often have about dogma and doctrine and present authentic Church teaching that is based on the Gospel of Jesus Christ and God's infinite love for creation?

Given most young adults' desire to help the less fortunate, how do we show them that their humanist attitude, while in itself commendable, has a deeper foundation based in the Christian anthropology of the human person: created in the image and likeness of God, fallen but redeemed, and destined for eternal life with God?

So many people comment that youth and young adults are the future of the Church. How can we show by our words and actions that the youth and young adults are actually the present of the Church?

What are some of the "traditional" devotions of the Church that can be adapted so as to appeal to the spirituality of young adults and how do we adapt them?

---

**Michelle Miller** *is the executive director for the National Catholic Young Adult Ministry Association. She began her career in young adult ministry as a Catholic campus minister at George Mason University then went on to be the program specialist for youth and young adult activities at the USCCB. She holds a M.Ed. in counseling and development from George Mason University, and is currently enrolled at the Washington Theological Union.*

**Brett Hoover** *was ordained for the Paulists in 1997 and in September 2000 he became the founding director of Paulist Young Adult Ministries in New York City. PYAM is a ministry of the Paulists designed to promote young adult ministry and outreach throughout the United States and Canada.*

# General Session

## DISCIPLES IN ACTION

Raymond Gerard East • *Archdiocese of Washington*

Director of the Office of Black Catholics • Vicar for Evangelization

God is good! Somebody say, *"All the time!"* All the time! Somebody say *"God is good!"* Because almost half of our Church in North America speaks or understands Spanish, *"¡Dios es bueno!"* Somebody say *"¡Siempre!"* ¡Siempre! Somebody say *"¡Dios es bueno!"* Let's give God a handclap of praise in this place today! *¡Un aplauso por el Señor!*

First and above all giving glory to God, who is worthy to be praised, you can say "Amen!" I send greetings to all our delegates to this historic North American Institute for Catholic Evangelization. I also send you greetings in the Lord from that great Catholic evangelist Sr. Francesca Thompson, OSF. Illness prevented her  from being here this week. I am honored to speak in her place, and I know you will join me in wishing her God's healthful blessings.

Listen now to the beginning of the holy Gospel according to John:

> [*En el principio existía el Verbo y el Verbo estaba con Dios y el Verbo era Dios.*] In the beginning was the Word and the Word was with God, and the Word was God. [*Él estaba en el principio con Dios. Todo fue hecho por él y sin él nada se hizo cuanto ha sido hecho.*] He

was in the beginning with God. All things came to be through him, and without him nothing came to be. (Jn 1:1–3)

Whatever has come into being found life in him, life that for humans was also light! [*En él está la vida, y la vida es la luz de los hombres; la luz luce en las tinieblas y las tinieblas no la sofocaron.*] You didn't hear me, Church! What has come into being in him was life, and the life was the light of all people. The light shines in the darkness and the darkness has not overcome it! (c.f. Jn 1:4)

[*Vino un hombre, enviado por Dios, que se llamaba Juan. Vino para dar testimonio, como testigo de la luz. Para que todos creyera por él. Aunque no fuera él la luz, le tocaba dar testimonio de la luz.*]

There was a man, sent by God, whose name was Tyrone. Tyrone was a member of our parish, and he came after Mass to talk to me about a problem. He was looking for the Word. He had just been to Mass, had heard the Word proclaimed, sung, and preached, had feasted on the Bread of Life, and he was still hungry. He was looking for the Word.

In the introduction to his Gospel, John the Evangelist calls Jesus the Word of God, the expression of God, the thought of God. Paul would call Jesus the splendor and the image of the Father, the *Logos*. But Tyrone wasn't looking for Jesus. A lifelong Catholic, he had already found Jesus, received him as Lord and Savior. Tyrone wasn't looking for *Logos*, he was looking for *rhema*—*dabar* in Hebrew—that Word that goes forth from the mouth of God, that dynamic, living, explosive Word that does not return to God empty, but accomplishes the purpose for which it was sent.

So we debated whether this Word could be found in the Catholic Church. A few weeks later Tyrone came to me one last time, to tell me that he had joined a church just a mile away, remarkably called Rhema Christian Temple. This church had welcomed him warmly, saw that spark in him, blew it into a flame, and called him to be a minister of the Word at Rhema. He became a disciple in action. (We'll get back to Tyrone a little later).

Let me introduce you to another disciple in action. Dr. Michael Kissinger, like Sr. Annette Turner on our panel, met Jesus at an early

age, in the Baptist Church. A gifted musician, and composer, he is direc-tor of the Vancouver Bravo Chorale. Like Annette, he came to sing the Lord a new song in the Catholic Church. His wife Maria is the minister of music at St. Joseph Parish just across the river in Vancouver, Washington, and he came from organizing the Vancouver Wine and Jazz Festival, to tell us about the Word made flesh, who came all the way down to dwell among us.

## THE WAY

*On bended knee He felt the shame, and on His back He bore the pain.*
*There on His head, He wore the crown they made for Him that day;*
*And then He led them to The Way.*
*He walked the road to Calvary, and gave his life upon that tree.*
*He cried to God, "Forgive them all for what they do this day!"*
*And then He led them to The Way.*

*[Chorus]*
*My Lord is a living Lord, and my Lord is a giving Lord.*
*My Lord is a loving Lord, forever, amen.*

*Laid in His tomb, they set the stone; they wept for Him, but left, alone.*
*When three days came, the angel said, "He is alive today!"*
*And it was then they knew The Way.*
*He lives today, as Lord and King; we lift our voice and to Him sing;*
*God's only Son, He gave His Life that we might live some day;*
*And join our brothers in The Way. [Chorus]*

—Words and Music by Michael Kissinger, © 2001.
Reprinted with permission.

Church, we are gathered here on this tremendous Catholic campus (Somebody say, "Go Pilots!") in the North American Institute for Catholic Evangelization, to commit ourselves, whatever our specific ministry, to form disciples in action. We have come to this unique, multidisciplinary gathering to *Go and make disciples.*[1] Like an old preacher I once heard say, "We're just nobody who came to tell everybody about somebody who wants to save everybody! His name is Jesus!"

Do you know him, Church? Do you know him for yourself? He came to his own. *Vino a su propia casa, y los suyos no lo recibieron, pero a todos qu lo recibieron, les dió capacidad para ser hijos de Dios* (c.f. Jn 1:11–12).

Jesus came to his own, and his own did not receive him, but all who have received him he empowers to become children of God, by Baptism in water and the Holy Spirit. Who here is baptized? It seems too good to be true! We

are members of the divine family! The *Catechism of the Catholic Church* says of Baptism:

After the invocation of the Holy Spirit, it becomes the efficacious sacramental sign of new birth: just as the gestation of our first birth took place in water, so the water of Baptism truly signifies that our birth into the divine life is given to us in the Holy Spirit.[2]

> *"At the same time that African American Catholics are encouraged to discover their past, let them be encouraged to retell their story for the sake of the present."*

*Here I Am, Send Me: A Conference Response to the Evangelization of African Americans and The National Black CatholicPastoral Plan* (Washington, DC: USCCB, 1989) p. 3.

Did you see that beautiful baptistery in the chapel this morning? "One faith, one font, one Holy Spirit make one people. No barrier can divide where life unites." Jesus Christ sends his Holy Spirit in the anointing we receive at Baptism. Jesus Christ sends that same Holy Spirit upon everyone who is baptized in his name. At Baptism we were anointed like Jesus, to be disciples. We were empowered to bring the Good News to all people, to go and make disciples.

*Go and Make Disciples* (GMD) is our national plan and strategy for evangelization in North America. Goal III of *Go and Make Disciples* follows upon the first two goals. Not only do we seek to stir into a living flame the faith of all Roman Catholics (Goal I); we also go beyond the Catholic family to extend that faith to all people in the United States (Goal II). Goal III calls us to "foster Gospel values in our society, promoting the dignity of the human person, the importance of the family, and the common good of our society, so that our nation may continue to be transformed by the saving power of Jesus Christ" (GMD, 117).

The Gospel is our starting point. We look at the mission of Jesus. Filled with the Spirit he goes into the wilderness for forty days and nights and is tested by the devil. He comes out of the wilderness like Moses, victorious. Again, filled with the Holy Spirit, he goes back to his region and begins to teach in the local synagogues. One Sabbath, at the beginning of his ministry, he returns home to preach in the synagogue where he was brought up. In the black Church we call this the "trial sermon." Listen! Wisdom! Be attentive!

Jesus journeyed home to Nazareth one day, entered the synagogue to pray on the Sabbath. There he took the scroll, unrolled it, and proclaimed, "The Spirit of the Lord is upon me, because he has anointed me to bring glad tidings to the poor. He has sent me to proclaim liberty to captives and recovery of sight to the blind, to let the oppressed go free" (Lk 4:18). Let the trumpet sound, proclaim the Jubilee! The Spirit of God is upon me.

Every eye was fixed on him; the room was hushed and stilled. And Jesus said to them, "Today this scripture passage is fulfilled in your hearing" (Lk 4:21). God has anointed me to comfort those who mourn. Let the trumpet sound, proclaim the Jubilee! The Spirit of God is upon me.

## GOD HAS ANOINTED ME

*Jesus journeyed home, come to Nazareth one day*
*Entered on the Sabbath to the synagogue to pray.*
*There he took the scroll, unrolled it and proclaimed:*
*"The Spirit of God is upon me."*

*[Chorus] God has anointed me to bring good news to the poor.*
*God has anointed me to comfort those who mourn.*
*Let the trumpet sound, proclaim the Jubilee*
*The Spirit of God is upon me.*

*Healing for the broken, sight for all who long to see*
*On the day of justice, God will set the captives free.*
*A year of favor from the God of liberty*
*The Spirit of God is upon me. [Chorus]*

*Every eye was fixed on him; the room was hushed and stilled.*
*Jesus said, "I come to bring the rein that God has willed.*
*On this very day this reading is fulfilled*
*For the Spirit of God is upon me. [Chorus]*

—Words and Music by Gary Daigle with Marty Haugen,
from *Feast of Life: Stories from the Gospel of Luke.*
Published by GIA Publications, Inc. Chicago, IL © 2000.
Reprinted with permission.

After that, Jesus traveled around Galilee healing people who had every kind of illness. He preached the kingdom of God with such passion and integrity that it got him in trouble. In fact, Luke tells us that immediately after this trial sermon, Jesus' own townspeople went to throw him off the brow of the hill (cf. Lk 4:29).

*Go and Make Disciples* states that "evangelization is not possible without powerful signs of justice and peace," and that "this goal means supporting those cultural elements in our land that reflect Catholic values and challenging those that reject it" (GMD, nos. 117–118). It's that challenge that gets us arrested or in trouble! It was the uncompromising fidelity to his mission statement that got Jesus crucified.

*Go and Make Disciples'* Goal III three stretches us even further. We Catholics should continually share the Gospel with those who have no church community and with those who have given up active participation in the Catholic Church, as well as welcoming those seeking full communion with the Catholic Church. I quote:

> People can know they are invited to experience Jesus Christ in our Church only if they are really and effectively asked and if adequate provisions are made for their full participation. We want our Catholic brothers and sisters to effectively ask and to really invite (GMD, no. 54).

I have three challenges for us this afternoon. The first is, "Work the plan." The second is, "Connect the dots." The third challenge is, "Just get to it!" Since we are all focusing our ministries through the lens of evangelization, my first challenge relates directly to the ministry of our Church with Black-American Catholics.

## Work the Plan

What do I mean when I say "Work the plan"? black Catholics have been in the United States since 1538 when they came with the Spanish to Florida and Georgia. In 1638 a black Catholic freedman, Mathias de Souza, was on the first town council for St. Mary's City in southern Maryland. However, not only did some bishops openly condone the institution of slavery and some religious orders own slaves, but the Church generally ignored the evangelization of enslaved and free black Catholics. In Catholic states like Maryland and Louisiana, this neglect affected fifty percent of the total population. There was no mission plan. The first and second Plenary Councils of Baltimore could not even agree that African Americans *had* souls, much less come up with a comprehensive plan for their evangelization and catechesis.

Black lay Catholics took charge of their own evangelization in 1889 when Daniel Rudd and a hundred laymen convened in Washington, D.C. for the first black Catholic lay congress in American history. Not only were they convinced that the Catholic Church offered the best hope for people of African ancestry in the United States, they firmly believed that only the Catholic Church could break the color line of segregation in this country. In four subsequent Colored Catholic Congresses held from 1890 to 1894, they outlined a plan for the evangelization of all black people in America. This would be accomplished through integrated schools, access to Catholic higher education, the elimination of racism in the Church and society, and the promotions of black priests and religious. There is no record of a response from the Church to this plan.

A virtual century of silence of the Catholic Church was broken in July 1989. As a result of the Sixth National Black Catholic Congress two years earlier, a national pastoral plan for the evangelization of black Americans was adopted in the plenary session of the annual meeting of bishops in the United States. Three more congresses and numerous documents by our black Catholic bishops have shaped and refined that plan.

We've now got the plan; it's magnificent and it's specific. Now we have to work it! That's the first challenge.

## Connect the Dots

The second challenge is to "Connect the dots." This is the Holy Spirit's work of unity; it is the part of evangelization that connects with the work of reconciliation. We don't do black Catholic evangelization in a vacuum. For example, black Catholic evangelization touches Hispanic Catholic evangelization in the same way that the ghetto touches the barrio in so many communities. Both of us have national congresses or *Encuentros* and both of us have national pastoral plans for evangelization. But in how many dioceses do those dots ever get connected?

Just as we use this NAICE gathering to focus our ministries through the lens of evangelization, we must realize that in the black Catholic community, the evangelization dot touches the liturgy and spirituality dots. Many black Catholics like Tyrone whom I mentioned in the beginning of this talk leave the Church because their parishes and liturgies seem, pardon the expression, DOA, or spiritually "dead on arrival." Rather than stay in the valley of dry bones, the Tyrones of our Church leave for the refreshing waters of vibrant worship.

For example, I don't think that it's too strong to say that we have a "911 emergency" when it comes to Catholic preaching. If you can't say "Amen," say "Ouch!" Our black bishops addressed this in their documents *Plenty Good Room* on liturgy and *What We Have Seen and Heard* on evangelization. We must connect the dots of dynamic preaching and spirituality and solid teaching and social justice to keep evangelization real in the black community.

May I make mention in this second challenge about ecumenism? If Goal III of *Go and Make Disciples* urges us to "foster Gospel values in our society," the magnitude of this task is too small to be confined to the Roman Catholic community. Societal transformation by the Gospel of Life is the task of all Christians. If we have really grown to distinguish true

evangelization from proselytization, then our Lutheran dot needs to be connected to the Episcopal dot needs to be connected to the Methodist dot to the Presbyterian and Baptist and Pentecostal dots, and so on.

You remember the old joke about Heaven? St. Peter is giving the celestial tour, and when he passes the Catholic room, he whispers: *"Shhh! Those are the Catholics. They think they're the only ones up here!"*

Gospel values in society will be fostered when Protestant and Orthodox evangelism programs connect with Catholic evangelization programs. Ecumenism will help us connect the dots necessary for a full realization of Goal III. The culture of death will be converted by the Gospel of Life when all God's children learn to "walk together children and not get weary for there's a great camp meeting in the Promised Land."

## Just Get to It

Finally, we evangelists need to "Just get to it!" We're at a critical moment in the history of American Catholic evangelization. The need to proclaim the Gospel of Life in the new evangelization seems to be greatest at a time when diocesan budgets are strained and our focus is on other priorities. We've seen diocesan offices of evangelization shrunk or folded. Parishes who once had evangelization committees have often gone on to the next "flavor of the month." NCCE, after twenty years, has folded its tent. Due to the enormous investment required for this historic NAICE gathering, I'm not sure whether we will be able to meet like this again. Still, we resist the urge to build three tents. Like the disciples on the Mount of Transfiguration we are called by Jesus to go back down and evangelize. Just get to it!

The thousands of black Catholics like Tyrone who have left our Church searching for the Word need us to "just get to it." The 2.4 million black Catholics who rejoice at a changed Church with Bishop Wilton Gregory's presidency of the USCCB urge us to "just get to it." The fifteen million inactive Catholics need us to "just get to it." Our youth and young adults and families need us to "just get to it." No excuses about diocesan budgets or your organization's mission statement. Evangelization must be at the heart of all that we do as Christians. Let's just get to it!

So the next time you feel like God can't use you, just remember:

Noah was drunk . . .
Abraham was too old . . .
Jacob was a liar . . .
Leah was ugly . . .
Joseph was abused . . .
Moses was a stutterer . . .
Gideon was afraid . . .
Sampson had long hair and was a womanizer . . .
Rahab was a prostitute . . .
Jeremiah and Timothy were too young . . .
David had an affair and was a murderer . . .
Elijah was suicidal . . .
Isaiah preached naked . . .
Jonah ran from God . . .
Naomi was a widow . . .
Job went bankrupt . . .
John the Baptist ate bugs and was fashion-challenged . . .
Peter denied Christ . . .
The Apostles fell asleep while praying . . .
Martha worried about everything . . .
The Samaritan woman couldn't get an anullment . . .
Zaccheus was too small . . .
Paul was too religious . . .
Timothy had an ulcer . . .
And Lazarus was dead![3]

So no more excuses, disciples in action. God's waiting to use your full potential to go out and evangelize. Let's just get to it!

1   United States Conference of Catholic Bishops, *Go and Make Disciples: A National Plan and Strategy for Catholic Evangelization in the United States. Tenth Anniversary Spanish and English Edition* (Washington, DC: USCCB, 2002)
2   *Catechism of the Catholic Church*, Second Edition (Washington, DC: USCCB, 1997) no. 694.
3   The "No Excuses" litany is by an anonymous author and was taken from the Internet.

**Raymond East** *was raised in San Diego and graduated from the University of San Diego with a degree in business administration. His position with the National Association of Minority Contractors brought him to Washington, D.C., where he later experienced a call to the priesthood and was ordained in 1981 by James Cardinal Hickey. Msgr. East served in six Washington parishes before being named director of the Office of Black Catholics and Vicar for Evangelization. He is a member of the boards of Jobs Partnership Greater Washington and Food and Friends. He also served on the boards of St. Vincent Seminary in Latrobe, Pennsylvania, and the University of Dallas. He has worked in the areas of liturgy, initiation, and evangelization.*

# General Session

## CREATING AN EVANGELIZING SPIRITUALITY

*Beyond Ecclesial and Theological Maintenance: The Search for a New Missiology Within a Secularized Culture*

Ronald Rolheiser, OMI

## Focusing the Problem: The Need for a New Missiology

It's no secret that we're having trouble passing the faith on to our own children. Our churches are graying and emptying. Many of our own children are no longer walking the path of faith—at least not public and ecclesial faith—with us. The most difficult mission field in the world today is in secular Western culture: the board rooms, living rooms, bedrooms, and entertainment rooms within which we and our children live, work, and play.

And there's something anomalous about all this. There is a spiritual Renaissance of sorts happening in the Western world. Life at the level of parish and church community have never been more finely tuned, more biblically literate, or more liturgically healthy. We have wonderful programs for nearly everything, a well-trained clergy, and a laity participating more and more in the ministry of the Church. For the most part, at the level of parish life at least, we're doing a lot of things right.

The problem is not, it seems, diocesan life or parish structure. We know what to do with someone who walks through our church doors.

The problem is that we don't seem to know how to get anyone who is not already going to church—including our own children—to enter those doors. We are better at maintaining church life than at initiating it, better at being diocesan ministers than at being missionaries.

What's needed today in the western world is a new missiology for our own, highly secularized, culture. What's meant by that?

## What Is A Missiology?

Jesus' last words to his disciples in Matthew's Gospel were a missionary invitation: " Go, therefore, and make disciples of all nations, baptizing them in the name of the Father, and of the Son, and of the holy Spirit" (Mt 28:19).

Traditionally, we have interpreted this Gospel to mean that we are to go out to faraway lands and foreign countries as missionaries. Indeed, we have a wonderful tradition on this.

Today, however, we are coming to realize that the most important and difficult mission field in the whole world is not Africa, Asia, Latin America, or Eastern Europe, but our own children, our own culture, our own secularized world. How can we be missionaries to our own children?

## Elements of the New Missiology

A good missiology contains a number of important elements. First, it must do a proper diagnosis: it must accurately and insightfully name the moment; read the signs of the times; and try to identify why present strategies are failing. Second, it must be prescriptive: it must try to outline a vision from theology that will help remedy the situation.

## 1. Naming the Moment

Why is it important to name the moment? Being able to describe something is both a political and a prophetic act, an act of defiance in the face of terror and an act of hope in a time that seems to be bereft of it.

We are asked to try see the finger of God in the ordinary events of our lives. What is the finger of God pointing to in today's secular culture and in today's church? How can we describe it?

## 2. Naming the Key Elements in Our Culture and in Our Church

What are some of the salient features of our culture and church that should be named in terms of missiology? I suggest three of them:

### Multi-generational

According to David Tracy, we live in a time when modernism, post-modernism, anti-modernism, and pre-modernism are all meeting within the same generation. Thus there is often no single answer to the question, "What do people need?"[2] Nor is there a single ecclesiology operating within a single parish or community. Robert Schreiter accurately asserts that, in effect, we are two and a half (ecclesial) generations of Roman Catholics living and worshipping together in the same church.[3]

### Unfinished

Have you ever watched a typical, moody adolescent interact with his or her family in public? Picture a sixteen-year-old girl in a restaurant with her parents and younger siblings. She's at the far edge of both the table and the conversation, ashamed of her family. It's obvious she's simply enduring her family with less than a subtle patience. Her speech, manner, body language, everything about her, suggests disaffection.

Yet we don't take her attitude all that seriously; it's common and natural. When you're sixteen, your family can do nothing right, you're ashamed of its faults, and your parents and siblings seem the prime agents blocking your freedom, potential, and growth.

What an apt image to describe how so many of us, wanting to be mature in a sophisticated culture, relate to our Judeo-Christian roots and its churches! Nurtured in a culture that was born out of a Judeo-Christian womb, many of us are at the edges of our religious heritage, hyper-critical about the religious family we've been born into, and convinced that our Christian roots are what stand between us and proper freedom, achievement, and enjoyment. Whether it is expressed or not, this is the spirit that underlies much of the anti-Christian, anti-ecclesial, and anti-clerical feeling within our time.

The intellectual disaffection with Christianity today is not bad. It's just unfinished. It needs to grow up more and become cognizant that the heritage of which Catholics are so critical is the very thing that has given them the freedom, insight, and self-confidence to speak all those words of criticism. We can learn something from the young thirty-something man or woman who is now carrying real responsibility and beginning more and more to appreciate the family heritage, despite seeing the family's faults. We see this all the time: the bitter, distrustful adolescent, mouthing criticism of the family from the edges, growing into a responsible adult grateful for how the family has shaped the adult soul.

The roots of feminism and many advances of the Enlightenment lie in the Judeo-Christian scriptures, which take as non-negotiable the values of individual freedom, democracy, equality of opportunity, and respect for others. It's no accident that these values have arisen so strongly out of Western, Judeo-Christian, culture. It has simply taken us a long time to understand more deeply the demands of our own heritage.

Secularity is not the enemy of the Church, it's our child, and the opposite of secularity is not the Church, but the Taliban.

*Mainstream*

We've reached a point in the Church in which our old imagination no longer serves us in certain places. In key ways, we have lost our "romantic" imagination (See the appendix). Our imagination still serves us in running diocesan programs, but is no longer functional in terms of making us missionaries.

Moreover, we live in a time when we are shifting from a Church of immigrant, poor, under-educated, and culturally marginalized members to a Church of affluent, highly educated, and culturally mainstream people. The situation, I suspect, isn't much different for most Protestant and Jewish communities. Our faith communities tend to work much better in immigrant settings than in mainstream society.

We need a new missiology for our secular culture. What might be the elements of such a missiology?

# From Maintenance to Missionary:
# The Search for The New Missiology

Elements necessary for a new missiology of the Catholic Church include the following:

- A new vocabulary for the faith for a post-ecclesial, secularized generation

- A new Gospel artistry to refire the romantic imagination of our generation

- A new way to reconnect the Gospel to the streets

- A new way to move beyond personal charism, effective preaching, and good theology to build lasting community

- A new construction beyond deconstruction

- A new evangelization of the culture's desire

- A new effort at being missionary rather than simple maintenance

- A new effort at finding common ground within a church and society that is highly polarized and very much given over to self-interest groups

- A new movement beyond the "baggage" of historical Christianity, which includes the "Recovering Christian" syndrome, sanctioned anti-Christian bias in our culture, and the view of Christianity as "tried and tired"

## Elements of an Evangelizing Spirituality

*Waiting in the Upper Room*

At the very end of the Gospel of Luke, Jesus sends his disciples into Jerusalem and instructs them, "I am sending the promise of my Father upon you; but stay in the city until you are clothed with power from on high" (Lk 24:49). The disciples follow his directive, enter the city, ascend to an upper room, and remain there in prayer and anticipation until Pentecost happens.

This is, I believe, Jesus' instruction to our generation of Christians in the secular world today. How do we stay until we are "clothed with power from on high?" By continuing to go to church meetings!

Keep this in mind: **Pentecost happened at a meeting!** One of the central events that shaped Christian history did not happen to an individual off praying alone or to a monk on a mountaintop or to a solitary Buddha meditating under a tree. None of these. Pentecost occurred at a meeting among a community, to a church congregation assembled for prayer, to a family of faith gathered to wait for God's guidance.

Moreover, it happened in a common room, a meeting room, in one of those humble, church basement-type of rooms. It is helpful to remember that our search for God should take us into public meeting spaces as well as private places of quiet and contemplation.

Where Christianity differs somewhat from most other world religions is on this very point. In Islam, Buddhism, Hinduism, and Taoism, spirit and revelation break into the world very much through the individual, particularly the individual who is deeply immersed in private prayer.

Christian spirituality and Judaism have no argument with that. There's a privileged experience of God that can be had only in private silence,

128

alone. To find God, to receive God's Spirit, sometimes we pull away from the group, set off to the desert, to the chapel, to the lonely place, to the quiet, to be alone with God. We see Jesus do exactly that. Mark's Gospel tells us that when his ministry was most intense, Jesus pulled away to be alone for awhile. There are times that call for withdrawal and silence.

In Christian and Jewish belief, however, there is an equally privileged experience of God that can be had only in a group, a community, a family, a meeting. We don't just meet God in the desert or in the deep quiet parts of our souls, for where two or three are gathered together in his name, there he is in the midst of them (Mt 18:20). In Christian and Jewish spirituality there are two non-negotiable places where we meet God: alone and in the family. These are not in opposition, but complementary, relying on each other to keep our experience of God both deep and pure.

Pentecost, it is important to note, happened to a group at a meeting, not to an individual alone in the desert. That can be helpful to keep in mind when we tire of meetings, despair of their effectiveness, or resent that they pull us away from important private endeavours. The setting of Pentecost can also be helpful in keeping us focused on why we go to all these meetings in the first place.

129

Meetings are the "upper room," the place where we wait for Pentecost. And what are we waiting for? Why are we in the upper room, at a meeting? Because we are waiting with others for God to do something in us and through us that we can't do all by ourselves; namely, create community with each other and bring justice, love, peace, and joy to our world.

And so we must continue to go to meetings. We need to spend time together waiting for God, waiting for a new outflow of heavenly fire that will give us the courage, language, and power we need to make happen in the world what our faith and love envision.

## The Invitation to the Rich Young Man

We are proficient in the spiritual life, beyond initial conversion, staunch and solid in grace. We're essentially good, prayerful, honest, decent, dutiful, generous, moral, and sincere persons.

But the operative word here is "essentially." We are these things essentially, though not radically. Like Abbot Lot, deep down we know that we're capable of more, that God is inviting us to more, but we are fixed at a certain level of mediocrity. Simply put, there are still too many compensations, addictions, and accommodations in our lives. As well, there is the fear of moving beyond what disrupts our lives. We live faith, hope, and charity to a point, and there was a time when that point seemed all that God was asking of us. Now, however, we sense a deeper call and know that we are being asked to let go of many things—both good and bad—to which we are clinging for comfort and stability.

This is precisely what Jesus asks of the rich young man in the Gospels, the one who had many possessions and "went away sad" Notice how the Matthew describes this young man as a person proficient in the spiritual life, essentially good, decent, honest, generous, faithful. But the young man also hears a deeper call, a clear invitation, a dissatisfaction with the level of his own generosity. "What do I still lack?" he asks. That's also our question (c.f. Mt 19: 16-22).

The poet Johann Wolfgang von Goethe wrote a poem entitled "*The Holy Longing*" in which, at a certain point in the spiritual journey, one is handed the invitation to become "insane for the light." What is this insanity?[1]

Jesus names it as the invitation to give up everything and follow him radically. Eventually we reach a point in the spiritual life when, precisely because we are proficient at being good and decent, we are invited like the rich young man in the Gospel of Matthew to give up our most cherished comforts and securities and plunge into the unknown in a radically new way.

## Re-Grounding Ourselves as Poor, as Children, as Virgins

Jesus tells us that we enter the Kingdom of God more easily when we are poor, childlike, innocent, and helpless. We had those qualities in abundance before we became affluent, educated, and sophisticated, but we had them by conscription, not by choice. Our helplessness came with our place in society.

Prior to having affluence, education, wide experience, and acceptance within the mainstream, we were innocent. Our innocence was a first innocence, our poverty a first poverty, and our reliance on God often dictated simply by our helplessness.

Faith and faith communities work well where poverty, naiveté, innocence, and helplessness exist. The Kingdom of God doesn't work nearly as well within affluent, sophisticated, and self-reliant societies.

The task for us then, however difficult, is to become post-affluent, post-sophisticated, post-critical, and post-self-reliant. We need to live willingly those qualities of poverty, innocence, and powerlessness that preceded our current status.

But how do we become those things? Our generation's job is to learn what the necessary characteristics mean, live them, and then pattern them for our children and others to follow. Each generation of believers must, like the Jewish prophets, eat the word of God, digest it, and give it its own flesh. Giving faith to others, especially our children, is not the simple task of handing on a treasure chest of eternal truths, like one

131

passes on a baton stick in a relay race. Each generation must first give its own flesh to those truths.

One of our major faith tasks, then, is to model a new way of being poor, innocent, chaste, and powerless inside of affluence, sophistication, experience, and the power and self-reliance these bring. The task of our generation of believers is to find and model that innocence which lies on the other side of sophistication.

# Appendix
THE NEED FOR A NEW ROMANTIC IMAGINATION
IN THE CHURCH: VOCATIONS

*The ideas expressed in this appendix are a preliminary study into Henri Nouwen's language and its evolution through the nearly thirty years that he wrote in the English language. They are not definitive at this point, but rather point precisely to the importance of a full study into his use of language.*

Shortly after he entered the Trappists, Thomas Merton wrote up the story of his conversion and journey to the monastery in a book entitled *The Seven Storey Mountain*. It became a bestseller that caught the romantic imagination of his generation. For years afterwards, Trappist monasteries were flooded with applications. A large number of men did become good monks because of a romantic ideal that Merton's story triggered.[2]

The absence of Merton's kind of romantic ideal is, to my mind, one of the main reasons why fewer and fewer men and women are responding to the call to priesthood and religious life in modern society. We need a new passion for the priesthood and religious life that people can fall in love with, something that inflames the romantic imagination.

Our sophistication, it seems, is killing us; we are openly weary and often cynical about these vocations. It is no surprise we get few takers. "No romantic illusions allowed!" seems to be the catch-phrase. If we applied that criterion to marriage, there would be few takers there as well.

Mature commitment depends upon wilful decision, and not upon naiveté, romantic feelings, duty, or lack of other opportunities. I very much like an expression used by Marriage Encounter groups that "love is a decision." They're right. We can, and often do, make commitments out of naiveté, lack of opportunity, or romantic feelings, but we won't sustain them long-term, at least not without resentment or infidelity.

We're mature only when we choose to love, serve, obey, bow down, give over our freedom, and give over ourselves to someone or something because we know and accept that this is the right thing to do, irrespective of how we feel about it on a given day or of what more attractive options might beckon.

But every romantic, mystic, or poet knows that first you have to fall in love! At some point after the honeymoon love has to become a decision, but that's not what initially brings a couple to marriage. First they fall in love, they get seduced by an ideal. That ideal turns out to be partly an illusion, but it's what's gives people the courage to give themselves over in the first place.

We need, again, to have a romantic ideal about the vocations to priesthood and religious life. Otherwise we can expect still fewer priests, nuns, and religious brothers in the future.

What makes for such a romantic ideal? What works and what doesn't? Mother Theresa's life, for example, fires the romantic imagination for some. She was a saint and her ideal of religious life, austere though it was, seemed wonderfully romantic. But why hasn't her vision led to a deluge of young women banging on convent gates in the Western world?

Perhaps more interesting for us in a highly secularized context is the ideal of religious life that is depicted in Sr. Helen Prejean's *Dead Man Walking: An Eyewitness Account of the Death Penalty in the United States* (New York: Vintage Books, 1996).[3] Her story has some key similarities to *The Seven Storey Mountain*. Both are confessional, artistic, morally attractive, subtly invitational, flattering of religious life, wonderfully romantic, and revealing of the hidden monk and nun inside each of us.

Both *The Seven Storey Mountain* and *Dead Man Walking* make priesthood and religious life a romantic vocation. Why hasn't the latter stirred up the same romantic fervor as the former? I wish I knew.

I would suggest that in the Western world today, our rectories, convents, seminaries, and monasteries are greying and emptying. Conservatives attribute this decline to secularity, to a lost sense of self-sacrifice, to an incapacity in many people to make a life-long commitment, to the sexual revolution, and to an erosion of faith in the culture. Liberals suggest other reasons: an emerging laity is heading the new spiritual vocations; an all-male priesthood and the ecclesiastically imposed discipline of celibacy need an overhaul; and the priesthood and religious life need to take on new forms before we can again in conscience call people into them.

There's some truth in all of these reasons, though none are the real culprit. What is? We lack a romantic ideal for these vocations. They've been subjected to a scorching exorcism and now we need to restore to them their angels, their proper light, their beauty. We need to re-romanticize priesthood and religious life and give people something beautiful to fall with which to fall in love again.

1   Johann Wolfgang von Goethe, "The Holy Longing" trans. Robert Bly in *The Rag and Bone Shop of the Heart: A Poetry Anthology*, eds. Robert Bly, Michael Meade, and James Hillman (New York: HarperPerennial, 1993), 382.

2   David Tracy, *On Naming the Present Moment: God, Hermeneutics, and Church* (New York: Maryknoll, 1994), 3-26.

3   Robert Schreiter, Comments made in a keynote address at the Oblate Symposium on *Being Missionaries to Secularity* (San Antonio: Oblate School of Theology, October 2-4, 2002). Proceedings to be published in 2004.

4   Thomas Merton, *The Seven Storey Mountain* (New York: Harcourt Brace, 1948).

5   Sr. Helen Prejean, *Dead Man Walking: An Eyewitness Account of the Death Penalty in the United States* (New York: Vintage Books, 1996).

# REFLECTION QUESTIONS

How would you define missiology? What elements would it contain? Why is it so important in our Church today?

"Secularity is not our enemy, it is our child; and the opposite ofsecularity is not the Church, but the Taliban." What does this statement mean and what are the steps to take to live in this world but not of this world?

Pentecost happened at a meeting! How can we get the most out of church meetings? Is there something we can do to embrace our meetings and to be proactive to allow the Spirit to lead us?

Father speaks of a "new flame." How is the call to the rich young man in the Scriptures a call to us in the Church today? What are the implications of this call?

---

**Ronald Rolheiser** *is the general councillor for Canada for the Oblates of Mary Immaculate. He is a community-builder, teacher, and writer with offices in Toronto and Rome. For most of his priesthood, he taught theology and philosophy at Newman Theological College in Edmonton, Alberta. He remains an adjunct faculty member at Seattle University.*

# General Session

## The Gospel and the Call to Mission

Donald Senior, CP

S ome years ago I read a Barbara Gordon novel whose mood and content have stayed with me. It was entitled *I'm Dancing as Fast As I Can* and was about the struggle of a very successful executive at CBS television. She had reached the pinnacle of her career as a major executive but under the impact of a frantic pace and extraordinary pressures her life began to fall apart—a shattered marriage, a terrible falling out with her daughter, and unaccustomed setbacks in her work. Gradually she sank into mental illness, literally locking herself away in her apartment, afraid to come out, nearly suicidal. The novel—which was based on a real story—deals mainly with this woman's struggle to put her life back together. One key moment came when in an excruciating bout of panic, she told her doctor that she literally did not know  how to live anymore—she was afraid to step out of her bed. The doctor said, "You do know one thing very important—you know how to breathe." And he asked the woman to be still for a moment and listen to herself breathing in and breathing out.

Years later, after a long steep climb to put her life back in order, the woman recalled that moment as a turning point for her. She did know how to breathe, taking in "life breath" and letting it out. This is the vital exercise that keeps a human being alive.[1]

That fundamental act—breathing in and breathing out—is a metaphor for what I am going to talk about this afternoon. This is a turbulent time

for our world and for the Church. In the midst of great vitality and blessing all around us, there is also much pain and loss, including the lingering and disquieting concern about terror that will never seem to end. Over the past few months we have been embroiled in war with Iraq and have almost lost hope about the prospect of peace in the Holy Land, the land of our ancestors in the faith. A lot of people find themselves checking the stock market these days to see where their retirement funds are going. And, of course, a scandal of sexual misconduct has scarred the Church and continues to raise profound and fundamental questions about its moral leadership.

Coupled with all this, many people who work in the Church feel themselves caught in a more subtle undertow that includes diminishment of numbers, budget cutbacks, uncertainty about the future, and low-grade depressions that suppress hope on the part of many and put people in a survival mode. We, too, may feel we are "dancing as fast as we can."

I am convinced that this is a time to resist such an undertow and to rediscover the fundamental inspirations that make us Christians in the first place. This, I believe, is the importance of a gathering like this where we reflect on the depth and beauty of our fundamental mission as Christian and Catholic people. It is really not a matter of being a Church that happens to have a mission but rather a mission entrusted to us as a Church. Recovering a sense of our fundamental mission is crucial for refreshing our spirit on a profound level. Extending Christ's presence into the world—in all of its beauty and depth, with all of its grace and transformative power—is the primary call of every Christian.

Evangelization or mission is not to be understood simply in the classical sense of mission *ad gentes*, although such a form of mission remains valid. No, we know that mission is not confined to the heroic ministry of a few who left their home shores to win souls for Christ. This is one of the great developments we can take pride in over the past few years—to have a sense of the full scope of the Christian mission in the world. Pope John Paul II has noted that every Christian " . . . has the prophetic task of recalling and serving the divine plan for humanity, as it is announced in scripture and as it emerges from an attentive reading of the signs of God's providential action in history. This is the plan for the salvation and reconciliation of humanity."[2]

Mission in this deep and broad sense includes witness and proclamation, a life of worship, prayer, and contemplation, a commitment to justice and peace, a respect for the integrity of creation itself, a commitment to interreligious dialogue, a respect for cultures and the obligation to acculturate Christian life, and a commitment to worldwide reconciliation in the midst of violence and divisions. Again quoting the Pope, the mission of Christian communities is to give witness "that dialogue is always possible and that communion can bring differences into harmony" (*Vita Consecrata: The Consecrated Life* [VC, 73]).

This comprehensive sense of the Christian mission is truly, in the pope's words, a "plan for the salvation and reconciliation of humanity" and of the creative world in which humanity thrives (VC, 73). Its spirit is not imperialistic or dominating. Even as the Gospel is proclaimed with confidence and with gratitude for its proven beauty, evangelization is done in a spirit of respect for others and their sacred traditions and the integrity of their cultures. The modalities of this sense of mission are dialogue, witness, and service.

## The Mission of Jesus and the Call to Christian Mission

It is a truism but let us repeat it here: every form of Christian life must take its inspiration from the life and mission of Jesus. This is firmly stated right at the beginning of each of the Gospels where the call to discipleship and mission is presented as a powerful invitation from Jesus himself. Who can forget in the opening chapters of Mark and Matthew's Gospels those encounters by the Sea of Galilee: fishermen Simon and Andrew casting their nets in the sea; James, son of Zebedee and John his brother, sitting in their boat mending their nets? They have no inkling of what is about to happen to them, something that will change their lives forever.

Jesus, walking by the sea, calls to them, "Come, follow me and I will make you fishers of men" (Mk 1:16–20). They drop their nets and leave behind the boat in which they had been sitting.

In Capernaum, the border town on the frontier between the realm of Herod Antipas and Philip, Jesus meets Levi, Son of Alphaeus, sitting at his tollbooth. "Follow me," is the unadorned command. And Levi gets up, leaves his counter, and follows Jesus. That night Levi and his tax-collector friends dine in celebration with Jesus, who earns a sharp rebuke from the religious leaders for associating with such unsavory characters. But Jesus does not flinch: "Those who are well do not need a physician, but the sick do. I did not come to call the righteous but sinners" (Mk 2:15–17).

The exquisite story of the call of Peter takes place in Luke's Gospel. Jesus' magnetic power draws to the shore of the sea a large crowd thirsting to hear his words. The crowd's eagerness presses Jesus to the water's edge, where some fishermen are washing their nets. Their boats are now empty after a nighttime of futile fishing. Jesus steps into Simon's boat and asks him to push off a bit from the shore, and in such a glorious pulpit Jesus of Nazareth preaches to the crowds on the shoreline in front of him.

When his sermon is finished, Jesus asks Simon to cast out into the deep and let down the nets for a catch. "Master," Simon replies, "we have worked hard all night and have caught nothing, but at your command I will lower the nets" (Lk 5:5). Such a catch he makes when he lowers the nets! The nets are tearing and the boats are in danger of sinking they are so full. Simon Peter, overwhelmed, falls down at Jesus' knees, "Depart from me, Lord, for I am a sinful man" (Lk 5:8).

Jesus responds, "do not be afraid; from now on you will be catching men" (Lk 5:10). When the boats straining with their cargo come to shore, Simon and his partners James and John leave everything and follow Jesus.

And in John's Gospel, the call to evangelize is not a command by the shore of the sea or at a tollbooth in Galilee, but in the Judean desert. While John the Baptist is preaching to his disciples, Jesus—the Son of God and Lamb destined for sacrifice—happens to walk by. "Behold the Lamb of God who takes away the sins of the World," proclaims the Baptist. Two of John's disciples begin to follow after Jesus, who then

turns to them and says, "What are you looking for?" This is a question that echoes down the centuries like a distant clap of thunder. "Master, where do you live?" they ask. "Come, and you will see," Jesus replies (Jn 1:35–39).

And so begins a chain of allurement. As Andrew returns to draw Simon Peter his brother to come and see what he has seen, as Philip, Nathaniel, and the two disciples of John the Baptist, all are caught by mysterious power of Jesus and leave everything to follow him.

There are many other stories of the call to discipleship, some with poignant variations. In the Acts of the Apostles, Paul is knocked from his horse on the way to Damascus, blinded by the brilliance of the Risen Christ, and called to be Christ's chosen vessel (Acts 9:1–16).

In perhaps the most moving story of all the New Testament, Peter's call is renewed at the end of John's Gospel. The deflated disciples are fishing listlessly on the shore of the sea of Galilee. They see a figure on the shore with a charcoal fire, someone unknown but hauntingly familiar. Once again, they are given directions on where to fish and once more bring in an abundant catch. Finally, there is the heart-pounding recognition of the Messiah, as Peter plunges into the sea and swims ashore. Jesus shares a breakfast of bread and fish by the sea with the disciples, who are caught in a mixture of joy and shame. The moment of reconciliation comes when Jesus asks, "Simon Peter, do you love me more than these?" three times, healing the breach of a threefold betrayal. When Jesus says, "Feed my lambs, feed my sheep," the discipleship of Peter is restored, the call renewed (Jn 21: 1–19).

Not all the calls to be disciples of Christ are heeded. A rich young man whom Jesus loves turns away because the cost is too high. A scribe seeking the truth about the commands of the law is close, but still a distance away. "You are not far from the kingdom of God," Jesus says to him (Mk 12:34). For Nicodemus, who dares to come to Jesus only by night, only the shattering loss of death will move him to overcome his fears and claim the body of the Crucified Christ (Jn 19:39).

What an ensemble of strange and wonderful encounters! We might note at the outset, the fundamental qualities of these stories:

- The stories make abundantly clear that the life of discipleship begins not with a choice, but with a *call*. It is Jesus who either by majestic command or compelling magnetism initiates the life of discipleship. His authority and his alone is the source of that call. It comes unexpectedly and without warning.

- The call is first and foremost a call to follow after Jesus. The focal point is the person of Christ, which remains the heart and soul of all Christian experience. The disciples follow after Jesus, surely not ahead of him and nor alongside him. It is an enduring image repeated over and over in the Gospels: Jesus is out in front of his community; the disciples follow behind, often in confusion and fear.

- The disciples who are called to follow Jesus also will share in his mission of redemption. They will be plunged into the work of transforming Israel, of renewing the covenant community, of establishing the kingdom, of healing and exorcism and teaching just as Jesus did. And their destiny will be to encounter the withering power of alienation and death in Jerusalem just as Jesus would.

- Lives of discipleship are changed forever. The disciples leave their boats, their families, their tollbooths. Once the call is heard, their lives fundamentally change and new allegiances are required.

If the Christian mission must take its spirit and meaning from the mission of Jesus, let me cite again the fundamental image of "breathing in and breathing out." That primal human function is also a metaphor that I think describes the fundamental character of Jesus' own mission as portrayed in the Gospels. I have come to think of his ministry like the

142

work of breathing—a drawing in of life to a vital center, the extending of life to the farthest boundaries of reality, a gesture similar to an embrace, a reaching out and drawing in. The more I conceive of Jesus' mission in terms of these two related movements, the more they become one fluid action and characterize the fundamental elements of Jesus' ministry: reaching out and drawing in. Both gestures were compelled by the deepest convictions and religious instincts of his life and his vocation: reaching out in a wide embrace of the whole expanse of Israel, including those on the margins; drawing in the entire community—washed and unwashed—into a communion of life that gives glory to God.

One of my favorite texts is Matthew 11:17–19, in which Jesus confronts his opponents, playing back their hostile words,

> 'We played the flute for you, but you did not dance, we sang a dirge but you did not mourn.' For John came neither eating nor drinking, and they said, 'He is possessed by a demon.' The Son of Man came eating and drinking and they said, 'Look, he is a glutton and a drunkard, a friend of tax collectors and sinners.' But wisdom is vindicated by her works.

Implicit in his opponents' hostile response is a tribute to the two characteristic gestures of Jesus I spoke of. As a "lover of tax collectors and those outside the law," Jesus has extraordinary outreach beyond the accepted boundaries of his day. Jesus was committed to restoring Israel to God. Hence, in a spirit of compassion, he sought out those who lived on the margins of the community, those on the fringe, the "lost sheep" of the house of Israel. And, at the same, time this "drunkard" and "glutton" drew in the lost to the vital center where he would break God's bread with them. Here we also see reference to the inclusive meals so characteristic of Jesus' mission as portrayed in the Gospels.

Both of these gestures—reaching out and drawing in—are fundamental to the Gospel portrayal of Jesus. No contemporary study of the historical Jesus would deny the fact that Jesus had extraordinary rapport with those on the margins, with those who were isolated and alienated. Think, for example, of the Gospels' emphasis on Jesus' commitment as a charismatic healer. All one has to do is read the opening chapter of Mark's Gospel to see in raw and powerful detail the story of Jesus healing from sunup to sundown, the doors jammed with the sick, who come

143

to him as if drawn by some magnetic force. Healing is not only physical transformation—and Jesus was surely dedicated to that—but healing also involves the dissolving of isolation and exclusion which the sick characteristically experience in society.

Virtually all of Jesus' encounters with Gentiles in the Gospel literature are in the context of healing. This reflects, in part, the inherent boundary-breaking nature of the healing stories in the New Testament. In most of the stories both the healer (Jesus) and the one to be healed perform a boundary-breaking movement, reaching across the chasms of taboo, culture, and indeed across the boundary between life and death itself in order to be healed. Healing has a comprehensive sense, involving not only physical transformation but spiritual, psychological, and social dimensions.

Language of liberation is often used in the healing stories, particularly when demonic possession is described as oppressive, as in the case of the Gerasenes demoniac in Mark 5:1–20 or the woman bent double in Luke 13:10–17. From the New Testament perspective at least, the Christian mission of liberation can find a profound basis in the healing mission of Jesus, which frees people from overwhelming experiences of evil that dehumanize and oppress them. Healing or exorcism results in liberation from evil and inclusion in a community of life.

The transformations involved in the healing stories include not only the physical, social, and spiritual condition of the sick or disabled, but also a profound challenge and transformation of the community itself. Thus in the story of the woman bent double in Luke 13, the liberation of the woman by Jesus is seen as a major disturbance to the order of the synagogue by the synagogue manager. Jesus vigorously champions the right of the woman, a daughter of Abraham, to be healed on the Sabbath.

The healing of the demoniac in Mark 5, an obvious mission story, brings chaos and disruption to the village when the demon enters into a herd of pigs and the Gentile demoniac is restored to full participation in his community. In the story of the healing of the daughter of the Canaanite woman of Matthew 15, it is Jesus himself who finds his assumptions challenged. His mission is no longer just to the lost sheep of the house of Israel; that this Gentile woman and her insistent faith have entered into the realm of his healing ministry (Mt 15:22–28).

144

> *"Evangelization happens when the word of Jesus speaks to people's hearts and minds. Needing no trickery or manipulation, evangelization can happen only when people accept the Gospel freely, as the "good news" it is meant to be, because of the power of the Gospel message and the accompanying grace of God."*

United States Conference of Catholic Bishops, *Go and Make Disciples*. Tenth Anniversary Spanish and English Edition (Washington, DC: USCCB, 2002), no. 19.

These stories tap into a powerful inclusive dynamic within the Gospel literature, a dynamic captured not only in the healing stories but in materials as diverse as Jesus' signature teaching on the love of one's enemies, his call to Levi and other social outcasts, his parables such as Luke 15 on the lost sheep, the lost coin, and the lost son, and his radical emphasis on the obligations of forgiveness and reconciliation in the community discourse of Matthew 18. In all of this material Jesus draws the outcast, the marginalized, the alienated, and the oppressed into the vital circle of the community, at the same time calling the community itself to conversion and openness. Healing—understood in a broad and inclusive sense—was an intrinsic part of the early Christian understanding of mission.

Consider, too, as part of the expansive nature of his mission, Jesus' eye for the socially marginalized: Levi at his tax collector's post (Mk 2:15–17); the centurion in Capernaum (Mt 8:5–13); the Canaanite woman (Mt 15:22–28); blind Bartimaeus by the roadside (Mk 10: 46–52); Zacchaeus in his sycamore tree (Lk 19:2–9). It is also clear from the Sermon on the Mount and other sayings and parables of Jesus that he was convinced that those devalued by others were themselves capable of heroic virtue. Jesus had great faith in the capacity of the human person for holiness and greatness.

There is no doubt that the historical Jesus reached out beyond the boundaries and that his provocative outreach was not confined to the boundaries of Israel. Jesus, it seems, opened his mind and heart to the occasional Gentile as well. As a devout Jew, Jesus did not frequent Gentile territories, but when confronted with one of God's children in need, even a Gentile, he responded with compassion. He set the foundation for what the early community would ultimately feel compelled to do—reach beyond Israel in the name of the Messiah. Jesus earned and gloried in the judgment of his enemies: "a lover of tax collectors and those outside the law."

Finally, there is the dimension of his "drawing in," which is an important way of understanding that Jesus did not come to found the Church in the sense of establishing a completely new entity apart from the community of Israel. The Church already existed as the *gahal* of God, as the assembly or *ecclesia* of Israel.

Jesus' vocation was the restoration of Israel, the breathing of new life and a deeper sense of community into the people in covenant with the God of Mount Sinai. Jesus, in a burst of wonderful irony and God-given optimism, called his ragtag band of disciples the Twelve and promised they would sit on the thrones of the twelve tribes of Israel.

Here, surely, is the inner meaning of the extraordinary meals that were characteristic of the ministry of Jesus. In each case, meals in the Gospels represented Jesus' mission as a gathering of Israel, as an inclusive communion of all the children of God, as a sign of the ultimate communion in joy and praise and abundant vitality with the God of Israel: meals with Levi and his friends, meals with Simon the Pharisee, meals with the crowds on the hillsides, meals with his disciples. The ideal meals are described in the parables: wedding feasts in which the invitations extend to the highways and by-ways; royal banquets groaning with food and seeking guests; meals at which strangers would come from east and west and sit at table with Abraham, Isaac, and Jacob; and Passover meals drenched with poignancy and longing.

These characteristic meals evoked for the early community the story of God feeding his people in the desert with manna and with quail, a sign of the Eucharist to come. In the vision of Isaiah 25, God would set a banquet on Zion and feed the people with choice meats and beautiful wines, taking away the cobweb of death and drying the tears from every face (Is 25:6–8).

The mission of Jesus, understood in these terms of outreach and drawing in, of inclusion and communion, would lead ultimately to his death and give meaning to the cross as an act of profound love. Jesus died because of the way he lived.

The characteristic notes and deep patterns of Jesus' ministry—his reaching out and his drawing in—can ultimately be traced to Jesus' own experience with the God of Israel. His was a God whose transcendent beauty reached far beyond the boundaries of Israel's imagination and far exceeded it hopes, a God whose unconditional love and startling compassion were more than any human heart could grasp. This God was the ground of Jesus' being and the foundation of his mission. The Spirit-driven intuition of the early community would enable it to see that Jesus not only revealed this God through his ministry but that Jesus himself—in his very being—embodied this divine reality.

Here we touch on another intuition of the Church's teaching about mission that has come to the fore in our times, namely that the ultimate theological and biblical foundation for mission is the very life of God, indeed the mystery of the Trinity itself. God embodies the mission impulse to reach out in self-transcending love. This is an incredible, irrepressible abundance surging out into the act of creation, love extending into the life of a people and their history. This is a love whose ultimate intent is to draw all creation into the unfathomable beauty and vitality of God's own being—to create a communion among all living things.

Here is the ultimate life act: breathing out and breathing in, reaching out and drawing in. This divine rhythm of life is the ground of all mission. In a wonderful book on mission in the Old Testament entitled *Unity and Plurality*, Lucien Legrand points out that this rhythm finds an echo in a dynamic tension in Israel's own life. Israel stretches between the twin poles of its election as God's chosen people and its historic interaction—perhaps we might even say mission—to the nations. Although Israel regarded its own status as unique and compelling, it also understood that the God of Abraham and Sarah, the God of Israel, was also the "God of the Nations." Inevitably, therefore, Israel had to deal with the nations—at times standing against its surrounding cultures in the name of religious purity, at other times interacting with the nations and absorbing fundamental aspects of their cultural life and religious structures, and still at other times experiencing the nations as instruments in God's own purification or chastisement of Israel.[3]

That dynamic tension between identity and outreach, between community and mission, between particularity and universality arches through the entire Bible, including both Testaments. Israel was caught throughout its history between its sense of election as God's special people, concerned with the demands of the covenant to build a community of justice and compassion, and its duty to the nations, those peoples who were also children of Abraham and somehow destined to be part of God's ultimate embrace: election and outreach, community and mission, breathing in and breathing out.

As I move along in life I find myself depending more on John's Gospel to capture what Jesus ultimately means. I think of John as stepping back from the complexity of the synoptic portrayal of Jesus and his mission, distilling it, and tracing in bold and direct strokes the ultimate meaning of it all. John's Gospel says it all, in a manner that is at once both simple and profound. John begins his Gospel with an exquisite hymn that asserts Jesus' ultimate origin in God. God speaks so eloquently, so completely that this word in fact, is *theos*. Because God wants to communicate— because God must breath out—the Word is sent by God into the world, penetrating the world's substance so completely that the Word becomes

flesh, becomes the Incarnate Word embodied in the world, with a human history, a human body, and a divine spirit. This, John dares to say, is the ultimate origin of Jesus. Jesus is the Word whose very flesh reveals God and God's message to the world.

If Jesus can be characterized as God's Word to the world, what is it that God wants to say in Jesus? What is the Word? John's answer is absolute and profound. No text says it better than John 3:16: "For God so loved the world that he gave his only Son, so that everyone who believes in him might not perish but might have eternal life." God's message is not one of condemnation, but redemptive love. This is the heart of the Gospel, this is what the Word has to say to the world, this is the primal evangelization.

For John, this ultimate message of God's redemptive love is expressed in every gesture of Jesus, every discourse, characteristic action, act of healing, prophetic word of truth, every relationship of Jesus with his disciples. All of this is ultimately a word of love, a word of life. That is why for John, the final and most eloquent statement of what the Incarnate Word has to say is spoken, paradoxically, through his death: "No one has greater love than this, to lay down one's life for one's friends" (Jn 15:13). John understands the death of Jesus as an act of friendship and love.

At the conclusion of his Gospel, John completes the circle. The final destiny of Jesus as the Word of God is ultimately communion with the God of love who sent him into the world. So John depicts the moment of Jesus' death as an ascent back to God, as a lifting up to the full communion of love for which the Word longs.

John's Gospel asserts that what happens to Jesus is also the destiny of humanity. Through the power of the Spirit, the disciples, too, are to learn the language of love, to love as Jesus did, to lay down their lives for their friends. And, as in the case of Jesus, so the ultimate endpoint of human destiny is communion with God, when all will be one.

Here is where the Jesus of history and the Christ of faith fuse into one. Jesus of Nazareth can be described as animated by God's presence, by an experience of the God of Israel as transcendently holy and awesomely beautiful. Yet this God is also infinitely tender and unconditionally gracious and loving. If this is the core conviction that imprinted itself in the character of Jesus' mission and teaching, then the Spirit of God has led the Church from its first moments to understand that *so completely did God's presence suffuse Jesus that he was that presence Incarnate*. So thoroughly did Jesus of Nazareth radiate the Spirit of God that he substantially partook of that divine Spirit. Jesus revealed God not only by his profound teaching but also in his very embodiment as the Son of God.

Not far is the bridge between the Gospel portrayals of Jesus and the Church's convictions about the identity of Jesus and the character of faith in him. We owe Paul the key insight that the Church is the Body of Christ, not just as an apt description, but as a profound metaphysical reality. As scandalous or as fragile as the Church community may appear, we believe that in and through the Church the Risen Christ is present, embodied, and visible to the world.

If the Church is the body of Christ in the world, then the actions of the Church and its mission must aspire to reveal the same fundamental character of Jesus Christ as portrayed in the Gospels. We cannot imitate Jesus on the level of the details of his life. We are not first-century Palestinians, charismatic Jewish healers, or messianic teachers. But on the level of fundamental character, of defining characteristics, there must be credible correspondence between Jesus' mission and the mission of the Church. Both the life of Jesus and the life of the Church have to be grounded in the character of the God revealed by Jesus, both have to be seated in the harmony that gives tone and coherence to everything we ultimately say and do.

## Conclusion

If breathing out and breathing in is a metaphor for the divine act in the world, if reaching out in a gesture of compassion and justice to the boundaries of human life and creation and drawing in to a vital communion of life and love defines the mission of Jesus, then this is also the fundamental mission of the Church and of every form of ministry within the Church. If the Church is to be the sacrament of the encounter with Christ, then this also defines the fundamental character of every Christian community whether a parish, a religious community, or any formal gathering.

A sense of mission that reflects the divine mission in the world and one in harmony with the mission of Christ is not just reaching out, therefore, but also gathering in. Far too often we wedge them apart and define mission only in the sense of crossing boundaries or turning inward to a stale ecclesial culture with no concern for, or vital communion with, the world of humanity and creation of which we are a part.

The scope of the mission to which we are called by the Risen Christ is, conversely, a mission rooted in the very life of the Triune God and one whose goal is the very quest for ultimate life and communion with God. The enterprise to which we are called is far more fundamental than any of our concerns and far more crucial than we can imagine.

This is something very important for us now. At a time of diminishment for many, at a time when we feel awash in scandals of the most debilitating kind, in a world whose uncertainties and explosiveness are threatening, we could think of our mission as hopeless or insignificant. We could, in fact, forget how to breathe.

No, we are not engaged in something petty or sectarian or trivial. We need to remind ourselves that we are alive. We are not simply leading pious lives or performing routine tasks. Our biblical heritage, the very wellsprings of our faith, remind us that we are called to partake in the divine task in the world, to reach out in healing and compassion to all of God's people, drawing in from across boundaries of culture and race and age to form a communion of life pleasing to God.

Even if we who are entrusted with the Church's mission are weak and inadequate, even if the way is not always clear for us, we are engaged in a noble, sacred task whose boundaries are as wide as the world and whose purpose is nothing less than the glory of God. We must remember that it is the tradition of our faith that God's Spirit is not confined to the Church but roams the world and its peoples breathing where it will. The arena of mission is not simply the Church but the world itself. "The field is the world:" these are Jesus' own words in his explanation of the parable of the weeds and the wheat in Matthew's Gospel (Mt 13:38).

So, despite our problems and our weakness, this is not a time for hesitation or retreat. We cannot submit to fatigue of the spirit. Now is the time to lift up our best and most noble and most ambitious ideals for ourselves, for the Church at large, and for the next generation of Christians. This is the moment to renew our sense of the Christian mission to the world, a mission whose purpose is no less—in the words of our pope—than the "salvation and reconciliation of humanity" (VC, 73).

1  Barbara Gordon, *I'm Dancing As Fast As I Can* (New York: HarperCollins, 1989).

2  Pope John Paul II, *Vita Consecrata: The Consecrated Life* (Washington, DC: USCCB, 1996), 73.

3  Lucien Legrand, *Unity and Plurality: Mission in the Bible*, trans. Robert R. Barr (Maryknoll, NY: Orbis, 1990).

# REFLECTION QUESTIONS

Which Gospel story captures for you Jesus' essential mission of reaching out to those on the margins and drawing them into a community that recognizes God as its center, like "breathing in and breathing out?"

Who are the marginal and the "Gentiles" of our day, and how can you as a disciple reach out to them?

How can you see in Jesus' mission a direction for overcoming hopelessness brought on by the scandals and uncertainties of our times?

---

**Donald Senior** *is the president of the Catholic Theological Union (CTU) in Chicago. He has also been professor of New Testament studies at the CTU since 1972. Having entered the Passionist Religious Congregation in 1960, he was ordained to the priesthood in 1967. Fr. Senior has written or edited numerous books and publications, and has served on many boards and committees. In 1994, he received the Jerome Award, given for outstanding scholarship by the Catholic Library Association of America.*

# General Session

## BREAKING OPEN THE WORD OF GOD

Susan Blum Gerding, Ed.D

Frank Desiano, CSP, D.Min.

## The Word is a Call to Conversion

I read a columnist who didn't like the phrase "breaking open the Word." He thought it was too trendy and perhaps violent. In fact, he once saw the phrase miswritten simply as "breaking the Word," and he thought that this is what people often did to the Scriptures: they broke them.

But the phrase is very helpful in one particular way: it shows that the Scriptures take a little more than just reading. It's more than moving our eyes over a page, and more than moving our lips and making sounds. Rather, the Scriptures have to be dealt with, grappled with, exercised, in order for us to truly take them into ourselves. Even when we have read the words and have them in our minds, we still have not really read the Scriptures.

Really reading the Scriptures will lead us to conversion, to change of heart and change of life, to experience the impact of God's Spirit in palpable ways in our lives. Perhaps we have a favorite novel or history book or analysis; perhaps we can talk about why this book is important to us and how it changed our lives. But the Scriptures are different still from these great reads—the Scriptures don't want to just change our lives or influence us. They want to transform us, to make us disciples, to lead us to ongoing and profound changes as the depth of God's love becomes clearer.

So at the Liturgy of the Word we do not read the Scriptures—we *proclaim* them. We read them out loud, showing that the Scriptures are not only about what's going on in our heads, but also what's going on in our lives, personally and as a community. We proclaim them, and we state that the Scriptures make a claim on us, make demands on us that we can avoid only at great risk.

What is the claim that the Scriptures make? They challenge us as we hear them, and they demand a response from us. The Scriptures are news—God's Good News—that ask us, as we hear them, what we are going to do as a result. Be it a parable, a prophet's cry, a miracle story, a confrontation between Jesus and his opponents, an image developed by Paul or Peter, or the Passion narrative on Palm Sunday, we can't just hear these words. We must respond.

So the Scriptures call and we respond. This is a process of conversion in which every liturgy involves us. We respond first of all in the Creed, which we as a community recite after we have heard the Scriptures read. This is our cry of faith. This is our voice saying, "I do believe, help my unbelief!" (Mk 9:24). This is the way we say that God is the center of our lives, that Jesus is Lord and Savior of all, and that we are obedient to the Holy Spirit of God.

We respond in an even deeper way by receiving the consecrated food of Jesus, his Body and Blood, taking Christ's dying and rising to ourselves as our own pattern of life. Because we proclaim the Scriptures, in the power of Jesus' spirit, we die to our old selves of sin and selfishness, and we rise as disciples who follow the path of Jesus. We take Christ into ourselves, pledging that we will live his life. "Yet I live, no longer I, but Christ lives in me": Paul's words are our spiritual biography (Gal 2:20).

We respond by our lives beyond the Eucharist. It is how we carry God's Word and Christ's Body into the world, into our families and neighborhoods, into our cities and workplaces, that shows the depth of our conversion in Jesus Christ. To hear God's Word in church demands that we live God's Word in the many sanctuaries of our daily lives.

## A General Method to Approach the Word

Is there a simple process for breaking open the Word, getting to hear it with power and freshness so that we can respond? Any process or technique must serve one primary purpose: to make the power of the Word come through so that we realize the urgency of responding and the claim God is making on our lives through the Scriptures.

We would like to offer a simple technique that might be appropriate to a variety of settings in which we break open the Scriptures, whether in preparing a homily, doing a personal meditation, or helping a group understand the Scriptures. This technique involves four questions:

- What is the Word saying about its setting?
- What is the Word saying to believers and the Church?
- What is the Word saying about the world?
- What is the Word saying to me?

The Word is saying something about the setting, the history, the community in which it arose, about the ancient Jews who are our ancestors of faith, and about the first Christians who formed communities and recalled the stories of Jesus. God uses human history, language, imagery, grammar, and community to reveal God's truth.

While we do not have to be historians or professional scripture scholars, it is important to try to grasp the setting because it helps us interpret what we are reading. Or, more importantly, it keeps us from misinterpreting what we are reading. Most modern Bibles with notes can help us understand the setting of the Scriptures.

The Word is speaking to us a community, as a Church and as a parish. The Word challenges us about the kind of Church we are and the ways we do or do not reflect Christ's ideals. How many of our parishes are stuck in one mode of action even as the Word calls us to become something else? How many times do we need to read about mercy and compassion, about welcome and generosity, to realize how cold, small, and uncompassionate we often seem as a Church?

The Word is also speaking about the world—both our local neighborhoods and the whole global setting of modern consciousness. What is it saying? How is it challenging the world and our culture, and how it is touching culture, to bring about changes consonant with the Kingdom? What does the Word say about us as a society, our values, our occupations, our priorities, our passions, our use of money or time?

And finally, the Word is speaking to me personally as a disciple, asking how I will respond, change, grow, and live as a result of God's addressing me through the Scriptures. It asks me about my relationships, particularly with God, and my vision of myself, my dreams and my fears, my ambitions and my humiliations. If we read the Scriptures aright, they will not leave us alone.

# Accessing the Word of God

When I first heard the phrase, "breaking open the Word of God," I also was not comfortable with it. For me it conjured up images of breaking something violently, like throwing a glass vase onto a tile floor and dumping all of the water inside onto the floor, or striking something very hard in order to open it. What immediately came to my mind is the way I hold a tube of crescent rolls or biscuits and bring it crashing down precisely on the sharp edge of my kitchen counter. Poof! The dough expands and is ready to bake.

In a way, that is exactly what happens: the Word *does pour forth* and *does expand* as it is loosed from its bindings.

Part of the charism of Isaiah Ministries has always been our belief in the *power* of the Word preached in parish missions. We *expect* the Word, the incarnate Body of Christ, not to return empty, but to act in our lives, in our homes, in our community, in our world. We do not view sacred Scripture only as words on a page, words that will teach and instruct us, inspire and guide us (they will), but we also consider them a powerful source of kinetic energy!

Just as the mighty waters of a powerful river are held back by a dam, potential energy is only converted into electricity when the dam lets loose and the raging waters burst through the turbines of the power plant. For you golfers out there, an excellent example of kinetic energy is Tiger Woods' back swing. When he lets loose his tightly coiled upper body and strong leg muscles, sheer power blasts forth as the club hits the ball.

Likewise, Scripture becomes active and powerful when the Word bursts forth from the printed page and is proclaimed, believed, and lived. As Fr. Frank said, "The Scriptures call and we respond." We are called to repentance, to faith, to holiness, and when we respond, conversion, transformation, and change occur. We have a choice and that is to respond or not to respond to the Word. We can choose to be apathetic about the Word, or ignore it, or just not listen.

So the question becomes, "How do we access the power of the Word in such a way that we *will* and *must* respond?" A question that I like to use

*"In fact there are innumerable events in life and human situations which offer the opportunity for a discreet but incisive statement of what the Lord has to say in this or that particular circumstance. It suffices to have true spiritual sensitivity for reading God's message in events."*

Pope Paul VI, *Evangelii Nuntiandi: On Evangelization in the Modern World* (Washington, DC: USCCB, 1997) no. 43.

is, "How can we make the Word come alive in our own lives, in our communities, in our world?"

I would like to suggest a way of accessing the Word that I have found very helpful in making the Word come alive for me, whether I am using it for personal reflection, for a presentation at a parish mission, or for helping groups better understand the Word.

I call it "Imagining the Scriptures." It is based on *lectio divina* [sacred reading] to a certain extent, but then takes off in a totally different direction. In the interest of time, I will presume that most of you are aware of the *lectio divina* process, which basically is prayerful reading of a Scripture text several times, listening for a specific word or phrase that touches you, reflecting on that phrase, and finally entering into contemplative prayer. In the process that I use, instead of listening for a specific word or phrase, I intentionally seek out a focal interest in the text that could be anything—a person, the setting, an inanimate object, an animal, a word or a phrase. And then I imagine that I am that focal object.

For instance, I have used this process and imagined that I was actually the woman at the well, the blind beggar, or the lost sheep. At other times, instead of being one of the characters, I imagined that I was one of the inanimate objects: the Star of Bethlehem, the empty wine jug at Cana, the rock at the entrance to the tomb, or even the tomb itself.

Once, I imagined that I was the phrase, "Forgive us our debts, as we forgive our debtors," and how that phrase yearned to be heard and how it felt about falling on deaf ears, not being heard, not being acknowledged, not being authenticated (c.f. Mt 6: 9). That image led to a realization of how important all words are and how open I must be to hearing them and how often I close my mind to the words of others in my family, in my church, in my community, in the world.

After reflecting on the focal object, whatever it may be, imagining the conversations, thoughts, or feelings of the character, object, or phrase, I ask the four questions which Father Frank suggested:

- What is the Word saying about this setting?
- What is the Word saying to believers and the Church?
- What is the Word saying to the world?
- What is the Word saying to me?

Let me give you an example. In today's Gospel, as you will see, Jesus is sending his disciples out two by two with certain instructions. Perhaps I would focus on the disciples and imagine that I am one of them. If I were Peter, for instance, what would I be saying to Jesus in response to his instructions? How would I feel? What would I do? Who would I choose to be my partner? What would I want Jesus to say to me?

Or, perhaps my focal point might be the walking stick. Then I would imagine that I am the walking stick. If it could talk, what would the walking stick be saying? "Oh, no, here we go again. Where is this man forcing me to go now? I'm tired. And I'm old and crooked." Or might the walking stick be saying, "Wow, what an opportunity to help the disciples go on their way. I may be old and crippled and I can't do a whole lot for them, but at least I can help them in my own small way."

Or perhaps my focal point might be the occupants of the house in the distance who see the two disciples coming. "Who are these two strangers? What do they want? Probably beggars. Look, they carry nothing except a walking stick, no suitcase. Maybe they are thieves. Oh, listen, they bring us tidings of peace, but preach that we must repent. Their message is not an easy one. Do you really think that we should let them stay here for a few weeks?" And what do you think they said when the disciples left their house, shaking the dust from their sandals after a few weeks' visit? Or what if I chose as the focal point the phrase, "Shake the dust from your feet" (Mt 10:1-20)?

The process of "Imagining the Scriptures" is basically that I carry on an imaginary conversation in my mind and then ask questions in relation to the four questions that Fr. Frank posed:

- What is this focal point trying to tell me in relation to its setting, to believers and the Church, to the world, to me?
- How does it feel to be this person/object/phrase in this Scriptural community, this setting?
- What is the main message that the focal point is trying to help me understand? Does it speak to my relationships with my family, my parish, my community?
- What have I learned from the focal point?
- How does this message (this new knowledge or understanding or insight) impact my family, my church, my community, my world?
- How will I change in response to this encounter with the Living God?

Normally, I write the responses to these questions in my journal and end with a prayer of gratitude.

IMPORTANT:  Sometimes this experience does not lead to a clearly defined teaching or insight, but instead leads to more questions or challenges, and becomes a conversation to be continued.

IMPORTANT:  In this method of breaking open the Scripture, the focus is not on the Scripture character or the inanimate scriptural object. The focus is on Jesus' mercy, love, forgiveness, compassion, commandment, whatever is revealed personally to me in this particular Scripture at this particular moment in time.

IMPORTANT:  The method I use is actually very simple, but it does assume a certain degree of basic knowledge concerning Scripture, the setting, the times, the situation, the community, the culture, and so forth for the sake of accurate interpretation. Prior to using this method, scriptural notes or commentaries may be explored concerning the text.

Later in this workshop, I will lead you through a guided experience of today's Gospel using this method. But first, let us listen to God's word, and then Fr. Frank will discuss the importance of the setting of the Gospel.

## The Scripture Readings

To Amos, Amaziah said: "Off with you, visionary, flee to the land of Judah! There earn your bread by prophesying, but never again prophesy in Bethel; for it is the king's sanctuary and a royal temple." Amos answered Amaziah, "I was no prophet, nor have I belonged to a company of prophets; I was a shepherd and a dresser of sycamores. The LORD took me from following the flock, and said to me, Go, prophesy to my people Israel (Am 7:12-15).

Blessed be the God and Father of our Lord Jesus Christ, who has blessed us in Christ with every spiritual blessing in the heavens, as he chose us in him, before the foundation of the world, to be holy and without blemish before him. In love he destined us for adoption to himself through Jesus Christ, in accord with the favor of his will, for the praise of the glory of his grace that he granted us in the beloved. In him we have redemption by his blood, the forgiveness of transgressions, in accord with the riches of his grace that he lavished upon us. In all wisdom and insight, he has made known to us the mystery of his will in accord with his favor that he set forth in him as a plan for the fullness of times, to sum up all things in Christ, in heaven and on earth. In him we were also chosen, destined in accord with the purpose of the one who accomplishes all things according to the intention of his will, so that we might exist for the praise of his glory, we who first hoped in Christ. In him you also, who have heard the word of truth, the Gospel of your salvation, and have believed in him, were sealed with the promised holy Spirit, which is the first installment of our inheritance toward redemption as God's possession, to the praise of his glory (Eph 1:3-14).

He summoned the Twelve and began to send them out two by two and gave them authority over unclean spirits. He instructed them to take nothing for the journey but a walking stick—no food, no sack, no money in their belts. They were, however, to wear sandals but not a second tunic. He said to them, "Wherever you enter a house, stay there until you leave from there. Whatever place does

163

not welcome you or listen to you, leave there and shake the dust off your feet in testimony against them." So they went off and preached repentance. They drove out many demons, and they anointed with oil many who were sick and cured them (Mk 6:7–13).

## The Gospel Setting

Every Gospel narration is also a reflection of the early Christian community in which the stories and words of Jesus are being remembered. These narrations come from specific settings in the lives of the early Christians. Their experience of community—what they recalled about Jesus and how they recalled it—shapes our communities today who hear their Gospel. God uses the experiences of early Christians to speak to all future Christian communities.

Mark is giving us some basic rules of evangelization in its explicit sense of announcing the King of God in the name of Jesus Christ. We hear instructions for the Twelve, those he called into his inner circle, as they set out on mission in Galilee, their home territory. Perhaps their success on this mission will lead them to expect similar results when they go to Jerusalem—perhaps.

We can feel the nervousness of these early missioners, how Jesus must tell them not to load themselves up with things or expending all their energy on that. They must most of all expend their energy on the message. Extra money, clothes, shoes only load you down.

We can also see the modes of hospitality in the early Church, how messengers would be accepted and given food and a room. Jesus tells his apostles to rely on that, and points out the dangers of using peoples' hospitality by running from house to house, looking for a better meal in the next house.

He also warns them against being discouraged if people will not hear their message. The disciples must wipe the dust from their feet, forget the failures and miscues, and go on to the next town, the next welcoming house, the next person who responds to the message of peace and healing.

Finally, we see the importance of deeds: praying, healing, conquering evil as a way to verify the message and apply it to peoples' lives. It is not enough to get the message right, it's not enough to speak it. Christ's message, God's Kingdom, must be done, shown, accomplished in actions.

Isn't this the perfect Gospel for a gathering about evangelization?

## Breaking Open the Word

As we break open the Gospel today, I would like to lead you in a guided conversation at your table. We have heard the Word, we have experienced a discussion on how important the setting is. Fr. Frank clearly identified several main points in today's Gospel:

1. the basic rules for evangelization
2. the nervousness and apprehension of the disciples
3. the modes of hospitality in that time
4. the Lord's warning not to become discouraged
5. the importance of deeds

In light of the setting, this guided conversation will be divided into four sections to discuss the question we posed earlier. To help you get in touch with your own thoughts and feelings, you might want to imagine that you are one of the disciples to whom Jesus was talking directly in this Gospel passage.

First, please share with your group the first question:

> What is the Word saying to the world today, especially considering the culture and environment? What would Jesus say to political, economic, and governmental world leaders today? (5 minutes)

> What is this Gospel saying to believers and the Church today? What do you think Jesus would say to the laity, priests, and bishops today? (5 minutes)

> What do you think this Gospel is saying to your parish today? What do you think Jesus would say to your pastor, your pastoral council, your evangelization council, the members of your parish? (5 minutes)

> What is this Gospel saying to you personally about your own attitude, fears, expectations, and hopes as an ambassador of Good News? (5 minutes)

Obviously, there is not enough time for you to discuss these questions thoroughly with your group, so please consider this exercise a "conversation to be continued."

Frank and I both want to thank you for your attention and we hope that our comments have been helpful as we "break open the Word," as we "ponder it in our hearts," as we release its energy and power, and as we respond to its call to conversion by living God's Word in our daily lives.

## Closing Prayer

Lord, in your love you undertook a journey from eternity into the midst of our history. Your journey came to its apex in Jesus Christ, who took on our flesh, lived our life, spoke our language, spoke out our hopes, comforted our fears, endured our death, and continued beyond death in risen life. We proclaim that risen life has been given to us through the Spirit of God whom Jesus poured upon us, making us disciples and calling us to continue the divine journey.

Lord, as our conference on evangelization draws to its end, we pray for your abiding Spirit in our lives, that we may continue the journey on which Jesus sent us as ambassadors of your divine life. May we bring your Word, may we embody your loving deeds. May we live for your Kingdom and make it our enduring message. May the world hear healing and peace from our lips and see them in our actions. May we be strengthened to carry on the journey until all are joined in your love. To this end, we raise our prayers:

1. That the Word of God will dwell deeply in the hearts of all men and women in the world today, we pray to the Lord.

2. That the leaders in our Church and in our parishes will hear the call to ongoing conversion through the Word, we pray to the Lord.

3. That the Holy Spirit will enlighten us as we "ponder the Word in our hearts," we pray to the Lord.

4. That, as believers, we may truly respond to the Word by living God's Word in our daily lives, we pray to the Lord.

5. That we may go forth from this convocation with greater conviction and skills to spread God's Good News, we pray to the Lord.

Recitation of The Lord's Prayer

The Sign of Peace

# REFLECTION QUESTIONS

As Fr. DeSiano says, "to hear God's word in church demands that we live God's word in the many sanctuaries of our daily lives." How does my daily prayer and daily living build the Kingdom of God?

Dr. Gerding says that "we are called to repentance, to faith, to holiness . . . and when we respond, conversion, transformation and change occur." How does my presence to the Word in prayer transform me? The community?

Of the many words we hear everyday, to what word is my heart listening? What word is shaping my actions?

---

**Susan Blum Gerding** *has been actively proclaiming the Good News through a variety of communication styles and methods since 1979. Dr. Gerding was the founding editor of* The Catholic Evangelist *magazine, and has written several evangelization training manuals, including the* Text, Study Guide, *and* Implementation Process *for* Go and Make Disciples *released in 1993 by PNCEA. Her most recent work,* Lay Ministers, Lay Disciples: Evangelizing Power in the Parish, *was co-authored by Rev. Frank DeSiano.*

**Frank DeSiano** *is a former president of the Paulist Fathers and is a consultant to the USCCB Committee on Evangelization. Fr. DeSiano was the principal writer of* Go and Make Disciples, A National Plan and Strategy for Catholic Evangelization in the United States *(1992). He is well known for his articles and books on Catholic evangelization and is a frequent speaker before clergy as well as national and diocesan gatherings.*

# Closing Liturgy

Archbishop John Vlazny • *Archdiocese of Portland, Oregon*

G rowing up Catholic on Chicago's South Side back in the 1940s and 50s was my first experience of discipleship. I don't recall ever hearing the word "evangelization" in our parish church, but even then I had a sense that somehow belonging to this church would involve being sent on mission, whatever that meant.

As I recall those days back at St. Gall Church, sometimes I now feel a little bit foolish. If your experience was anything like mine, you too were probably thrilled as a youngster when sister chose you for a special job at church or school, no matter how menial. I recall being happy over the prospect of collecting empty milk bottles, cleaning the blackboard, or sweeping the floor! Those sisters were very clever. When they wanted us to perform some of the most servile chores, they would have us believe it was a privilege for which we were specially chosen.

God too makes his choices. As St. Paul reminded us in today's second reading, we are God's chosen ones. As Paul wrote, "as he chose us in him, before the foundation of the world, to be holy and without blemish before him" (Eph 1:4). As a people, a Church, we realize that we all have been chosen to carry out the saving mission of Jesus in the world today. It is this awareness which has brought us together this week for the North American Institute on Catholic Evangelization.

I know that the early founders of the Church here in the Northwest took their evangelizing responsibilities quite seriously. And so do we. Here we trace our roots back to the Catholic community of Canada.

Our first archbishop, Francis Blanchet, arrived as a missionary from Québec back in the autumn of 1838.

Like Archbishop Blanchet, like Amos in today's first reading who was also called by God to prophesy to his people, each one of us is similarly chosen for something unique and special (Am 7:12–15). We cannot become discouraged or paralyzed by the conflicts of life. Great people typically experience rejection by the so-called experts of their time. Their strength and eventual success come from their faith in God and their trust in his call.

There was a second grade teacher who encouraged her pupils frequently to write letters to God. Little Norma has just visited the zoo and so she wrote: "Dear God, did you mean for a giraffe to look like that or was it an accident?"

This is a good question that many of us ask about a variety of things including giraffes, especially about events in our own lives. Today, particularly through the writings of St. Paul, God assures us that we are all part of a plan. Our lives are no mere accident. The Church we serve is just another sign of God's providential plan to be with us when we need him and even when we think we don't. This Church is no accident. It is God's doing—as we are.

I find it interesting that Amos, the shepherd and tree-trimmer-turned-prophet in today's reading, brought some rather troublesome news to the unjust and oppressive King Jeroboam who had conquered Israel. Amos was famous for giving warnings against the rich and self-secure of Israel. In today's reading, Amos is dismissed from the King's temple and told to go back to where he came from and mind his own business. Amos responds quite simply by explaining that he has been called by God (Am 7:12–15).

Not everyone will be enthused about our evangelizing enterprise, but we must imitate the simple posture of Amos and acknowledge humbly and confidently that we assume this task because of our call from God.

Today's Gospel relates the first of Mark's stories about the mission of Jesus Christ to all of Israel (Mk 6:7–13). Jesus invited the apostles to

READINGS
Amos 7:12-15
Ephesians 1:3-10
Mark 6:7-13

share that mission then, and today he invites us to do the same. Their task and ours is to confront evil in its spiritual and physical forms. But to do so, we must unburden ourselves of the "wrong stuff" of sin, selfishness, and alienation in order to stand up and be counted for the "right stuff" of health, healing, and repentance.

You and I can be owned by no one or no thing except by the blessing of God's choice and amazing grace. In fact, unless we learn to live more sharply, others—the unborn, the disabled, the poor, the elderly, the sick—will simply not live. This is a hard message. But it is true and it must be shared.

It has been a joy to celebrate out Church's evangelizing mission with you during these days here on Portland's favorite bluff. I dare say we all feel a little more pleased about who we are as disciples of Jesus Christ, we are more committed than ever to become a truly welcoming community of believers in our Catholic family, and we are energized to leave this place with a renewed commitment to build up the Kingdom of God wherever our journey of faith leads us in the months and years ahead.

Like the disciples of old, my sisters of brothers, we are indeed being sent on mission. Jesus Christ himself was sent by the Father to be out "sender." But before being sent, there must first be an encounter with the Lord so that there might indeed be an evangelizing encounter with God's people.

During this closing celebration of the Eucharist we once again meet the Lord. We pray that Catholic people everywhere will come to a better understanding of their call to share in God's plan for the salvation of the world. We ask that we ourselves will truly delight in being God's chosen ones. Then and only then will we be able to accept God's evolving plan for us lovingly and humbly.

My sisters and brothers, I think we've got it—we're going to go and make disciples!

---

**John G. Vlazny,** *archbishop of Portland in Oregon, attended the North American College and the Pontifical Gregorian University in Rome. A native of Chicago, he was ordained a priest in 1961 and remained in Rome, where he earned his S.T.L. from the Pontifical Gregorian University in 1962. In 1983 he was ordained by Cardinal Joseph Bernardin as auxiliary bishop for Chicago. In 1987, he was appointed bishop of Winona, Minnesota and served there until 1997, when he was appointed the tenth archbishop of Portland in Oregon. Archbishop Vlazny serves on several USCCB committees, and from 1993-1996, he was chairman of the Committee on Evangelization.*

# Remarks at Closing Banquet

Bishop Octavio Ruiz Arenas • *Diocese of Villavicencio, Colombia*

## Dear Brothers and Sisters:

Over the past few days that we have been gathered in Portland, we have had the opportunity to reflect upon Jesus' missionary mandate: "Go into the whole world and proclaim the Gospel to every creature" (Mk 16:15). The Church has worked to fulfill this task for twenty centuries, thanks to the action of the Holy Spirit and the evangelizing enthusiasm of thousands upon thousands of men and women who have accepted Jesus into their lives and have conveyed their wonderful experience to others by their word and life witness.

All of us, without exception, have received the same message through someone who loves us and has been willing to share the best of their lives: our parents, our siblings, a friend or perhaps a stranger whom somehow has motivated us to search for Jesus.

This has been the Church's perennial dynamic: that those who receive the message and find the Lord cannot remain quiet and keep that gift to themselves. On the contrary, they have to joyously proclaim that Jesus Christ has given meaning to their lives, that he has filled their heart with hope because they have experienced our Father's compassionate love in him who desires and calls us to eternal salvation.

This gathering on evangelization has been a wonderful experience of the universality of the Church. We've listened to the witness of bishops, priests, women religious and lay people, men and women. It has been presented from this North American culture, but the Hispanic, African and Asian presence has been seen and heard as well. We have shared different languages, but above all, we have listened and spoken the language that believers have in common: love.

Two bishops from Colombia, another bishop from Honduras, and two priests from Mexico and Costa Rica have experienced that love directly, through the cordial invitation to this gathering and the cordial welcome from all the organizers. Thank you for allowing us to have this wonderful experience, which we would like to replicate in our respective countries.

Like the disciples on the road to Emmaus, we have felt our hearts burning when we heard and perceived Jesus' presence in the midst of the evangelizing enthusiasm of each and everyone of you. This goes to show that we are before a Church that is alive and filled with Jesus.

Let me say a few words about an essential aspect of the evangelists themselves. We have to acquire the effectiveness of Jonah, the prophet, but we cannot imitate his arrogant attitude. Indeed, even after Jonah had lived his personal salvation in the whale's belly, Jonah preached as God requested—practically against his own will—and invited the people of Nineveh to convert. After three days, the unexpected occurred: everyone believed Jonah and did penance. But rather than being happy for the effectiveness of God's Word, Jonah became infuriated against our Lord. He wanted God to destroy this pagan and sinful people instead. Jonah was also afraid that his preaching would be ridiculed. The prophet did not understand that even divine threats are also a call to welcome

God's compassion and love; in other words, what was important was not the fire that would destroy the city, but that burning flame of God's love that transformed the hearts of Nineveh's citizens.

As evangelists, we have to imitate Paul's attitude. Upon his personal encounter with the Risen Lord, he felt that his life should be directed to conveying his experience. He felt that he was carrying a great treasure in clay vessels. He was convinced that he sowed, someone else watered, and that it was the Lord who produced fruit. And so, the greatest honor that an evangelist has is that others may recognize Jesus himself through the words of the evangelist.

On behalf of those of us whom have come from Latin America, I want to express my gratitude, first of all, to our Lord God who has called us to share this Church and who has allowed us to come to this gathering in Portland. We are grateful to the United States Conference of Catholic Bishops and particularly to the Secretariat for the Church in Latin America, which through its director Daniel Lizárraga sponsored our participation. Thank you Archbishop Vlazny and Father Tyson for your cordial welcome: you have been magnificent hosts. We thank each one of you for making us feel like your brothers at all times during these past few days.

*"Integration is not to be confused with assimilation. Through the policy of assimilation, new immigrants are forced to give up their language, culture, values, and traditions and adopt a form of life and worship foreign to them in order to be accepted as parish members. This attitude alienates new Catholic immigrants from the Church and makes them vulnerable to sects and other denominations."*

*Hispanic Ministry: Three Major Documents*
(Washington, DC: USCCB Publishing, 1988), 66, no. 4.

# Muy queridos hermanos y hermanas:

En estos días que hemos estado en Pórtland hemos tenido la oportunidad de reflexionar sobre el mandato misionero de Jesús: "Vayan a todos los pueblos y anuncien la Buena Nueva." La Iglesia ha cumplido ese encargo durante 20 siglos, gracias a la acción del Espíritu Santo y al entusiasmo evangelizador de miles y miles de hombres y mujeres que con su palabra y su testimonio de vida, han aceptado a Jesucristo en su existencia y han comunicado su maravillosa experiencia a los demás.

Todos nosotros, sin excepción, hemos recibido el mismo mensaje a través de alguien que nos ama y ha querido compartir lo mejor de su vida: nuestros padres, o nuestros hermanos, algún amigo o quizás algún desconocido que da alguna manera nos motivó para buscar a Jesús.

Esta ha sido la dinámica perenne de la Iglesia: quien recibe el mensaje y encuentra al Señor no puede quedarse callado y guardar para sí mismo ese don, por el contrario, tiene que ir a proclamar con gran alegría que Jesucristo le ha dado sentido a su vida, que El ha llenado a su corazón de esperanza, porque en él ha experimentado el amor misericordioso del Padre, que quiere y nos llama a la salvación eterna.

Este encuentro de evangelización ha sido, pues, una experiencia maravillosa de la universalidad de la Iglesia. Hemos escuchado el testimonio de obispos, sacerdotes, religiosas y laicos, hombre y mujeres; se ha hablado desde esta cultura americana, pero igualmente se ha visto y escuchado la presencia hispana, africana y asiática. Hemos compartido diversas lenguas, pero sobre todo hemos escuchado y hablado la lengua común de los creyentes: el amor.

De manera muy directa dos obispos de Colombia, otro obispo de Honduras y dos sacerdotes de México y Costa Rica hemos experimentado ese amor, a través de la cordial invitación a este encuentro, por medio de la amable acogida de todos los organizadores . . . Gracias por habernos permitido tener esta maravillosa experiencia que quisiéramos repetir en nuestros países.

Como los discípulos de Emmaus hemos sentido que nuestro corazón ardía al escuchar y percibir la presencia de Jesús en medio del entusiasmo